DOG TRAINING:

HOW TO UNDERSTAND YOUR FOUR-LEGGED FRIEND

BY:

Arthur Mood

and will not be liable to any kind of legal proceedings.

All rights still belong to original writers, and you quoted it here just to make this text more reflective and informative. The presentation of the data is without a contract or any type of guarantee assurance.

Logos got published without bothering any authority and utilized in the same manner. Logos employed here are all for clarification purpose, and real ownership of these logos still belong to real publishers and owners.

BOOK DESCRIPTION

If you are passionate about dog training, then this book is for you. In this book about our four-legged friends, we give you an introduction to dog training and what this training consists of.

Whether you plan to dedicate yourself to it professionally or are looking for professional techniques and solutions for your dog, this guide to training can be extraordinarily useful in understanding communication with dogs. You will easily find out everything you need to know about the introduction to dog training through this piece. Taking dog training is a great way to improve communication with dogs and deal directly with any problems you may have.

This training allows you to train dogs of all ages, provided they are in good physical and mental health. This book details everything you need to know about dog training in stages. Each dog has a particular personality and it is very important to know in detail his character in order to apply one technique or another, to require more or less complexity.

Various problems are linked with dog training. Many people find it difficult to educate and train their pets. To help with this, this book also offers you a complete guide to problems in training to help you discover what is wrong with your sessions and why your dog does not respond positively to education. Remember that a dog is not a machine, and that certain health or stress problems can have a very negative impact on training.

You have to take these points very seriously, and this is the reason why you need to go through this book. If your dog has started to show behavioral problems, it will be essential that you start working on correcting canine behavior as soon as possible. However, depending on the severity of the case, it would be ideal to contact a professional, whether an ethologist or a canine educator. On many occasions, we can confuse the different types of behavior, which makes us make mistakes in treatment. The guidelines proposed by a professional will always be the right one for a concrete case. However, this book also will help you to control all behavioral variables surrounding your dog, so rest assured, you can follow all the illustrations and guidelines in this book.

Table of Contents

CHAPTER ONE

The Criteria for Choosing Your Future Dog

It is essential to carefully choose the companion who will be by your side for the next ten or even twenty years! To make a good choice, you must:

- Choose a type of dog breed that goes in line with your lifestyle
- Choose a dog breed according to your needs
- Choose the kind of physical appearance that you like the most
- Choose a dog that is compatible with you
- Spend time with Fido

Above all, you must select your future companion according to the time you can give him and the activities you want to do with him.

The examples cited below are given for information only. Depending on each canine individual, the variables may change.

Examples of Dogs with Low Energy Levels

A four-legged friend with a low energy level will need to exercise for 45 minutes to 1 hour per day to maintain good health. These breeds of dogs might be of interest to you if you are a stay-at-home person or a busy person and want to take care of a dog who has a mild and calm personality.

- Greyhound
- Akita
- Bulldog
- Chow Chow
- Drogue de Bordeaux
- Neapolitan mastiff
- Pug
- Sharpei

Examples of Dogs with Average Energy Levels

These dogs are perfect for active people who have a lot of time to devote to their pets. A dog with average energy levels will need to exercise for 2 to 3 hours a day to be healthy.

- Labrador retriever

- Golden retriever
- German shepherd (except working line)
- Italian greyhound
- Chihuahua
- Standard poodle
- Shiba Inu
- Saarloos wolfdog
- Welsh corgi

Examples of Dogs with High Energy Levels

A dog with that has a high level of energy must exercise for 4 to 6 hours daily.

- Belgian Shepherd Malinois
- Jack Russell terrier
- Boston terrier
- German shorthaired pointer
- Siberian husky

- Border collie
- Australian shepherd
- Pitbull
- Beauceron

The Physical Appearance of Your Future Dog

For some owners, their dog's appearance is of paramount importance, while others have no problem with having the ugliest dog in the neighborhood. Here are some criteria that you can take note of when choosing your dog's appearance:

Do you want a small, average, or large dog?

Do you prefer short or long-haired dogs?

Do you wish to care for the pet's coat?

Would you like a dog with an athletic, elegant, or beefy physical appearance?

There are four categories of canine morphology:

- Mimosoids: Saint Bernard, Pug, Bulldog, Argentinian Mastiff, etc.

- Braconids: Brittany spaniel, Labrador, Saint-Hubert, Weimaraner, etc.
- Graybodies: Whippet, Saluki, Greyhound, etc.
- Loopoids: Husky, German Shepherd, Border Collie, Malinois, etc.

The Perfect Dog Does Not Exist

If you do not have a lot of experience but have fallen in love with a breed with a lot of character, it would be a wise decision to contact a dog training professional to guide you during the preparation of your dog.

Just like humans, all dogs have their weaknesses and their strengths.

Despite all your research and all your efforts, it is possible that the dog you have chosen does not have all the qualities you had been looking for.

…What then? The important thing, after all, is to create a relationship based on respect and complicity.

Why not visit a shelter? You could fall in love with a cute crossbreed dog!

Choosing the Perfect Puppy from the Perfect Breeder!

Unless you make a humanitarian adoption or offer a second chance to an animal, we all want our next companion to come from the best possible place. Now, finding the right breeder for your future dog (or cat!) is not an easy task!

I know, I have been there five times! I made four good choices and another ... pretty questionable one. I almost got caught, but I recognized the signs in time! In addition to my five breeder animals, I have one shelter dog. In short, I am starting to be quite experienced in the art of "shopping" for a future companion on all fours.

When you don't know exactly what questions to ask, finding suspicious breeders (also called backyard breeders) in the right places can be quite tricky. To help you and to demystify everything, let's talk together about the reasons why a dog breeder has a good reputation, and another one does not.

Why Buy a Puppy from a Good Breeder

If you are reading this chapter, you probably already know why you want to choose a good breeder for your next friend. For the needs of the cause, let's recap together why it is essential, if you do not want to adopt a shelter dog, to choose a good breeder!

To put it simply, let's explain what taking the time to choose the right place to adopt your future puppy saves you:

I don't buy puppies (or kittens) from suspicious sites, because I don't like:

- To spend a fortune on veterinary care. Animals from poor breeders very often have equally poor health.
- That my animal may not have a good structure. An animal that comes from a place with questionable conditions will often have equally doubtful joints—Dysplasia, dislocation, ligament problems, etc. I prefer to avoid all these inconveniences for my future dog!
- That my new dog may have a whole host of behavioral issues. If the breeder does not take great care in the selection of breeding dogs, you risk big: fear problems, aggression, bites, separation anxiety, and so on! If you breed two anxious and reactive dogs, you will have anxious and reactive puppies! Besides, a lousy breeder will not take the time

to give the puppies the best start. In addition to having lousy genetics, they will be isolated and under-stimulated, which is very bad for the socialization of your future puppy.

In short, I don't like my dog's suffering, both mentally and physically. I want the best for them, and it starts with the selection of parents through a program of socialization and mental stimulation.

The Four Basic Criteria

When I choose a breeder, I have four basic criteria. Follow these to put an end to inconveniences now!

- Parents of my puppies must be registered
- Parents of my puppies must have completed breed-specific health tests
- The parents of my puppies must be titled
- My breeder must breed puppies with a socialization and stimulation program

Am I picky? Yes! And I say it with pride. A dog will be part of you for up to 15 years. With the enormous progress in veterinary medicine, you could even speak of 20! Remember the points above. Do you want to have a dog that suffers physically and mentally for 20 years? I sure don't. You like to make wise choices too, and let's be proud of it!

Let's see together why these criteria are so critical, even if they seem superficial!

Are Papers, Titles, and Tests Essential?

There are a lot of shelters overflowing with animals who are just waiting for their family for life. Why, when thousands of animals hope every minute of their stay that someone chooses them, should you breed dogs?

It's a great question. The one I ask myself every time I choose a breeder. Why encourage someone who creates even more dogs?

Because it reproduces the cream of the crop. And if I'm not going to open my heart to one of these dogs or cats that fall asleep each night in their cage and say that they may be luckier the next day, the parents of my future puppy will be the best on the planet.

A breeder does not breed to sell puppies. He produces dogs to preserve a breed. Breeding improves and maintains a genetic heritage that would otherwise be lost. That's why a real breeder breeds. And to do this, dogs must be registered.

"Ok" you will tell me. "This dog is registered. He is purebred. Can you breed it?"

My following questions: What has this dog accomplished? What did he do? If you are to add even more dogs to Earth, there must be a reason. For a dog to deserve to be bred so that it can be justified to bring more puppies into the world, the dog must represent its breed, and thus, officially judged by a third party.

That is to say; this dog must have been presented in competition and stood out. Because, this dog, and this dog only, has something precious in its genetic heritage to keep. That's why it takes titles. Not to make it beautiful.

Then, it must be confirmed that the dog that has something that deserves to be preserved, and does not have other less glorious features that it could accidentally give to its offspring. Hence the importance of health tests. Diseases can be insidious, and extensive testing is needed to track them down. Each breed has its problems, and, for this reason, there are specific tests to be done for each of them before breeding a dog.

With the thousands of dogs and cats in full shelters, it is useless to add a litter of sick puppies! A visit to the veterinarian for a general examination is not sufficient. It takes extensive tests, like those listed by the OFA (Orthopedic Foundation for Animals).

Once all these exams have been done, then you have to do them again ... with the other parent. Proceed to mating. And once the puppies are born, give them the best possible start. My last two puppies were educated with the Early Scent Stimulation, Early Neurological Stimulation, and the Puppy Culture socialization programs.

I loved the results. My puppies arrived at my house with the best possible start, which made the adaptation very easy. It's all well and good to create good puppies with stable genetics, but you have to build on this foundation. We all know that socialization is essential. And it starts well before eight weeks!

To conclude, never hesitate to ask to see pedigrees, Orthopedic Foundation for Animal tests, and dog ribbons when you speak to a breeder. A real breeder will show them to you with great pride. A bad dog breeder will give you an evasive answer…

The Traps to Avoid When Choosing Your Dog Breeder

I explained all this to you, but you already knew it vaguely. Maybe not exactly, but you had a general idea. The problem is that once you present yourself to the person who calls himself a breeder, these individuals always seem to have the right arguments to make you doubt your position.

Do not panic! Here is the list of pitfalls to avoid and their counterparts! If you hear this, run away! Don't even take the time to respond. Take your belongings, smile politely, and go.

"I don't need papers; I reproduce balls of love."

"No problem with the papers. It's $700 without the papers and $1,500 with. Do you still want them?"

The most classic scam! This person breeds dogs without any papers and has given you such a huge discount that no one will ask for the documents. Did you know that recording papers costs… $ 30? We are far from an $800 difference here!

"My dogs are good dogs."

See the argument of balls of love. Dogs in shelters, too, are good dogs.

"Contests are scams. I never win because I don't know the right people / I don't bribe / etc."

There are lots of clubs and different types of contests. If one is not suitable, they can find another. There is no reason to reproduce an animal that does not represent its breed because there is no genetic heritage to preserve.

Terrible backyard breeders don't all come in the form of a filthy, awful-smelling plant. Sometimes they're a nice person with a clean living room who think they do well — someone who breeds the crossbreed of the moment. There are plenty of crusaders in the shelters. We are talking about justifying breeding a dog because it has unique qualities to preserve.

If you are giving your money to a bad breeder, you are telling them to continue their business.

I do not encourage puppy mills and backyard breeders. There are a ton of dogs in shelters that come from these places. If you want to save a dog, keep it there! You will do a good deed by not encouraging anyone to cause more animals to suffer.

Take a kindergarten class with your puppy and then an obedience class! Give it the best possible second start. Socialize it thoroughly. Take out insurance if your veterinarian determines that he is not in optimal health. If necessary, meet with a dog trainer.

I repeat, it happens. Now you know it, and they won't take it back! Refuge or breeder, what matters is the relationship between you and your dog.

Here! You all know my secrets now. Like real breeders, I have nothing more to hide. If I could sum it up, I would tell you this:

"A breeder dog doesn't mean that he is just a dog; it is the legacy of generations of work behind this puppy. A shelter dog is not just a dog, it is a second chance for you and this doggie. What matters is not where the dog comes from, it is the informed decision that you make before you go looking for it. "

Love your dogs, no matter where they come from.

Tips for Adopting a Puppy

Are your nights hell? Do you think you've adopted a shark?

He exhausts you, frustrates you ... and above all, you do not know where to start with him?

Pay Attention to Your Puppy's Health

The first months following the adoption of your puppy will be the most important regarding the diet and health of your furry companion. Indeed, during its first months of life, your dog grows (it will reach half of its final weight at the age of 5 months) and develops its immune system.

Choose the Right Food for Your Puppy

The kibble you choose must contain enough fat, protein, vitamin A and vitamin D. Also, be sure to select a holistic food, free of fillers such as corn and soy flour. Holistic food should only contain ingredients that provide benefits to your dog.

Choose a method of cooking with steam or low temperature rather than by extrusion: the latter method of cooking food removes a lot of nutrients.

The First Visit to the Veterinarian With Your Puppy

The puppy, like the child, has a weak and developing immune system. Your puppy is sensitive to outside bacteria and viruses that can cause kennel cough and deadly diarrhea. Also, young dogs more easily catch intestinal parasites since they swallow everything that passes under their noses. Beware of toxic foods and human drugs that are potentially dangerous for dogs!

The first vaccines your veterinarian gives your puppy will help prevent your new companion from contracting such illnesses.

If your puppy is not gaining weight and seems sick, his intestines may be parasitized by worms. In this case, a dewormer prescribed by an animal health professional will eliminate them.

Having a Dog: Facing Countless Responsibilities

Our customers often compare having a dog to having a child ... And that is far from false! Indeed, you will have to ensure that your doggie behaves well in society, that he can be obedient no matter the circumstances, and that he is healthy… Which of these points differs from the responsibilities that you have towards your children?

What is a well-trained dog?

Dog training: a way to develop a harmonious relationship with your dog

Dogs are our link to paradise. They know neither evil, jealousy, nor discontent. To sit with a dog on the side of a hill on a beautiful afternoon is to end up in the

Garden of Eden, where doing nothing is not boring ... it is peace.

A Well-Trained Dog is Happier than Others

It is much more pleasant to have an obedient and well-educated dog. And beyond the advantage that this gives to the master, trained dogs are happier than the others. They are less likely to fight with other dogs and tend to socialize better when they come across other dogs.

Having a well-trained dog is especially important if you have children in your family or your neighborhood. In the same way that a well-behaved child brings joy to those around him, a well-educated dog is a source of happiness for the home.

The time you spend raising your puppy is not wasted: it is a precious investment, and will affect the companionship you can have with your dog for the rest of his life.

Taking the time to train a dog will strengthen the bond that unites you and will assure you a long and happy friendship, which will benefit both of you. If you consider the time you spend with your dog, the time spent in training is very little and well worth it.

Basic Dog Training Orders

There are orders in dog training, and mastering them is relatively simple. These commands are as follows, and a well-trained dog will necessarily know them:

Sit: This is one of the fundamental orders of dog training, and one of the most useful for controlling your dog if he is rowdy.

Stay: This order is essential to ensure that, no matter where you are, your dog will stay in the place where you have decided.

Down: With this order, you will make your dog lie down on command. This is one of the basic commandments for successfully training your dog.

With me: This is the order so that your dog does not pull on his leash and walk at the same pace as you when you take him for a walk.

No: This is a particularly important word for your dog, and it can save you a lot of trouble. Reinforcing your dog to that word is one of the essential things in successful learning.

Training Your Dog Will Strengthen Your Relationship with Him.

If you go further than these fundamental orders, there is no doubt that this will only strengthen the relationship and understanding that exists between you and your dog, and consequently, the happiness that you will find in your moments together. It is well worth the time you will spend initially.

Training your dog will also allow him to understand that you are the leader, which will automatically eliminate many behavioral problems. Dogs that are not trained or poorly trained are often depressed and unhappy, and they display symptoms of anxiety. With dog training, you give a purpose to the life of your canine friend, and he will be happy to make you happy.

CHAPTER TWO

How to Properly Train Your Dog

Like children, dogs need to be well cared-for to feel good about themselves. An environment where the rules are absent or applied randomly will make your dog's behavior unstable and will cause several anxiety-related behavior problems. Also, you should never forget that rewarding a behavior randomly is the best method to maintain it.

So, be sure to systematically adopt the same responses to your dog's behavior to carry out his education or behavioral therapy. This will prove to be tedious, but it will pay off!

Your Dog Needs to Be Supervised

First, write down the rules that you think are important for living harmoniously with Fido. For example:

- Do not jump on guests
- Come when called
- Do not bark when someone rings your doorbell
- Sit when asked

- Wait to exit when you open the door

Second, systematically use the same vocabulary and the same gestures to guide Fido towards the desired behavior. If several people live under the same roof, it would be useful to arrange to get together and analyze the terms you use with your dog.

Keep one thing in mind; don't use repetitive commands to your dog ... He could quickly become confused:

"Sit—I said, siiiiiiiiit—sittttt—sit!"

"Come-my-dog-over-here-my-Kiki—Come!"

Ten Fundamental Training Tips for Running with Dogs

Many runners dare to go jogging with their dogs, enjoy the experience, and contribute to their pet's exercise. The benefits are multiple, not only for your dog but also for you. Especially if you go alone through the woods, since, in case of an accident or an injury, your dog will surely lend you a hand. Or a leg, in this case.

After sharing my experience with other dog owners who go out to exercise with them, you have concluded that there are several guidelines or previous tips that must be considered before going for a run with your dog. In addition to being positive for both parties, these outings will also help strengthen ties with your pet. Of course, first of all, you have to keep in mind that going out for a run with him should not and will not replace the daily walks he should do. Dogs are runners by nature. They go everywhere running. And, compared to us, they have several advantages. They do not become obsessed with any GPS or with the average pace, the burning of calories, or the total distance traveled, to name just a few variables. They do it for the pleasure of running. Because they have a good time, enjoy it. And you can join this enjoyment.

Dogs Can Help Us Maintain a Healthy Routine of Running

The fact that dogs are animals of fixed customs can help you keep a robust method of going for a run. Before going for a run with them or joining an organized race, there are many essential guidelines and points to consider and value.

• **Consult with a specialist.** In this case, the veterinarian. As in the case of sedentary people who start running after a long time without doing anything, before starting to run with your pet, you must consult with a veterinarian who will explore and assess their health to make sure that running with him cannot be counterproductive to his health. Some veterinary clinics and specialists advise that this check be done annually. Wow, that starts to seem just like the annual review that every athlete should do.

• **Not all dogs are ideal for running.** Not all breeds of dogs have the same physical characteristics and, therefore, not all are ideal for running and sports. In this sense, dogs with an elongated snout and a considerable size are ideal for running. Small, flat-snouted, and short-legged specimens, on the contrary, will prevent you from advancing with a certain rhythm, either because they do not have an ideal stride length or because they may have trouble breathing (which is what happens with dogs with flat faces). In this sense, a bulldog or a pug may not be the best running companion, unlike a pointer or a pointer.

• **Run with a special leash.** The same leash that you use to go for a walk with your pet will not help you jog with him. You must buy a technical, flexible strap that is attached to your waist. In this way, you can run hands-free and more naturally, and your dog will pull you off-course. In addition to being more comfortable, this form of anchoring will make your dual training safer. Thus, the ergonomic harness is essential to not limit the movements of your dog; in addition, it will be much less harmful than a collar. Most belts of this type have a maximum length of two meters, and at your waist, you will have a full and padded strap that will also prevent chafing.

• **Be patient.** If your dog is less than one year old, it is not appropriate or advisable to train with him. If you have a puppy, you can save this idea and try it again after a few months. You should wait until your dog reaches adolescence so that it can develop all its muscles and joints fully. As in the case of children, hard training at an excessively early age can be counterproductive to their normal development and negatively affect their musculature and skeleton. This waiting time usually ranges from 6-7 months (in the case of small dogs) to 12 months (in large dogs).

• **Begin step by step**. Once this waiting requirement is met that your pet is a minimum of one year old, it must also have a little more endurance. As you would not think of running 25 kilometers at a moment's notice if you have never completed more than 5, that is the case of your pets also. We must make a gradual increase in canine running time. Therefore, the adaptation phase is essential to enhance its resistance, and, with the passing of the weeks, you can make reasonably longer departures. Thanks to this continuous training, you can make the routine of running, little by little, also part of the daily life of your dog. On this note, it should be added that the timely progression in your sessions will also help your pet's foot pads to harden correctly, and this will prevent damage and subsequent injuries. After an outing in the mountains or through dirty terrain, it is recommended to wash the pads with soap and a cloth. Cleaning the dirt will prevent this sensitive area of the dog from becoming irritated and reduce the chance of infections.

• **Heat is not a good friend of fatigue.** With high temperatures, people have a hard time and you must control your hydration even more. The same thing happens with dogs, with added difficulty. They stick out their tongues and gasp to cool down. They do not sweat on the skin, like humans, and their thermoregulation capacity is even less effective. Therefore, it is important not to go running when it is scorching, since they do not resist heat in the same way as you do. If you expose them to high temperatures, they can have a collapse, heat stroke, and even death. Therefore, with temperatures above 75-80 degrees Fahrenheit, you should always be cautious.

• **Hydration and food.** This point is closely linked to the previous section. You must always go jogging with your pet accompanied by a bottle of water, unless you know with absolute certainty that you will find sources on your trip. Of course, you have to wait for the dog to stop panting for water. You must wait for him to calm down since if you give him water when he is panting, he also swallows air, something that can involve excessive stomach dilation— something even more significant in large dogs. As for food, it is best not to feed your dog for an hour before and one hour after the session. As in the case of a person, eating the hours before or immediately after exercise can lead to gastric problems or even swelling of the stomach.

• **Consider the running surface.** Like people, the different surfaces you run on also affect dogs. Dog pads are ready to run anywhere, although it is also true that some surfaces are better than others. Also, if your dog has a considerable weight and is not very used to going through the forest, it is advisable to smear his legs with a special cream when you go with him to run on roads and mountains (there are several different creams in the market that help to harden the pad of your pet). In this sense, you should avoid running on asphalt and excessively hard ground, especially if you are not used to it. Soft soil, grass, or sand on the beach would be the most suitable areas for this.

• **Maximize enjoyment** ... You must understand that going out to train with your pet is a new scenario for them. But these types of outings are not going to replace your workouts, nor should you take them as part of your development for any particular career.

... And enjoy the rest.

Just like us, dogs can't go running every day without stopping. You have to learn to rest, and this is part of the whole training process. As you do yourself, you must gradually increase its outputs. If you correctly follow this process, you will surely establish a new relational stage between the two of us.you

If you get a new pet, you must strive for their care. With a dog, you must also educate it properly to learn the basic rules of coexistence

Choosing to have a pet at home is undoubtedly a brilliant decision, and that is one of the best ways to complete a family. However, you must bear in mind that you must pay attention to both their care and their education, and for this, we are going to offer you some advice thanks to which you hope you can decide as useful as possible in your particular case.

One of the main problems that you may encounter when you have just adopted a dog is precisely the fact that it makes more mess than you would like.

If you live in a remote area, then you only have to have a little patience, since you will gradually get used to it and, in short, it will also moderate its barking except in very particular cases.

However, if your dog fails to adapt or if you are in an area where you might be disturbing your neighbors, then obviously you have to do everything in your power to control these barks in the most effective and fastest way make it possible

But in any case, you must be aware of how crucial it is to train your dog, especially if you start when they are still young and have a personality that can be molded in a much more effective way.

You can choose to access a course or platform through which to inform you about

Puppy Training, which is a beneficial investment since in a short time, you will see that you are getting your new partner to adapt without problems to its new living conditions you have with your family.

Remember that starting with practical and realistic training will be the best way to adapt the animal to its new life, while also avoiding many problems and, above all, you can enjoy its company to the fullest.

But if you like animals, if you are considering dedicating your future to it, then there are many alternatives for you to start moving in this direction. For this, you can start by trying an online dog grooming course, an excellent way to begin to take the first steps, thus getting to know some of the essential details and start to build a foundation as effectively as possible.

The next step will be to add training in other different areas, but always following the path of what you like and attracts attention, be it dog grooming, the veterinary care, etc.

For example, here you can take courses about horses where you can go taking your first to gain knowledge in the field of the horse. In the same way, we suggest you keep in mind the many alternatives that you have at your disposal, opting for those thanks to which you vsm start learning the necessary information to reach all the knowledge that allows you to lean in the shortest possible time.

With these resources, we hope you have found everything you need to take care of your dog and educate him properly, and of course, also to be able to change the course of your life and start doing something that fills you.

Also, your dog will be inclined to further respect the limits you impose on him and to obey the commands you ask him. He will know that whenever you order him to do or not do something if you stay true to your decisions and persist in enforcing them.

Environmental Management: The Key to a Successful Dog Education

If your dog is exposed to one of his phobias or sources of reactivity without you being present or ready to manage the situation, this could make your pet more aware of this source of stress.

So be sure to manage your environment well:

- Cover your windows if your dog tends to bark when he sees people

- Cage your dog if he tends to urinate on your floor
- Keep your dog on a leash if it jumps on guests

Make sure you maximize your chances of success and that of your dog.

In short, you will manage to build an affinity based on respect that will be as rewarding for you as it is reassuring for your dog.

Read on:

Dog training is based on different techniques that have evolved and which consider the needs of the dog and the training objectives.

Dog training or training is based on different techniques that have evolved and which consider the needs of the dog and the training objectives. Training the puppy is crucial because it is often synonymous with safety.

For example, if your dog later escapes on a walk, if you taught him the command for 'come' you wouldn't have a hard time bringing him back to you before it is too late. Of course, there are dogs with behavioral problems. If this is yours, a behaviorist can help. But before you panic, know first that dog training is a job that takes place over time. Do not be discouraged!

Some Training Methods

- The lure. With a treat, you help the dog to achieve the desired behavior. For example, you raise the gift above the nose and towards the dog's ears to sit in a movement that is normal to him.

- The clicker. After teaching the dog the meaning of click, you will guide it by clicking/rewarding each step towards the desired behavior. For example, to show the dog to go lay down on his cushion, you will click/reward few times: when he looks at his bed, goes to bed, touches the bed, and puts his four legs on the bed.
- Capturing. You reward the dog when it spontaneously assumes the desired behavior. For example, when the dog goes to bed instinctively, say "down" and give him a treat. After a few exercises, he will have understood that lying down on command will be rewarded.
- Limitation. This method is based on social learning. A particular protocol teaches the dog to imitate the actions of humans. For example, picking up an object, carrying a sachet ...

During training, the word you link with the behavior must be spoken when the dog offers this behavior and not before, since the dog does not yet know it. When the dog has learned the exercise, you will say the chosen word (sitting, lying, in the basket ...) to give it the order.

Some Training Tips

- The rewards must be adapted to the dog and very motivating. To teach a new exercise to the dog, choose kibbles, industrial treats, fresh food, all low in calories, or a toy that he adores, according to his preferences.
- Regardless of the training method chosen, the dog must not be handled or physically restrained. Otherwise, the dog seeks to flee from an unpleasant situation and will not learn to propose the behavior spontaneously. Training must be motivating for the dog to increase its reliability.
- Do not say "no" to the dog when he is wrong. This word is often used only when the dog does something stupid. Be forgiving and patient.
- Do not use restrictive or painful training accessories such as choke or electric collars.
- Work in short (no more than 15 minutes) and regular (several times a week) training sessions to see progress, especially if you train a dog that is still very young.
- Do not ask your dog about things that he is not yet able to do because

you could demotivate him. Be progressive and patient.

Environmental Management During Dog Training

During your training exercises, you can modify your environment so that your dog is less distracted or less likely to adopt prohibited behaviors:

• Put a barrier in front of the bedroom door if you want it to be banned.

• Place boxes or a chair on your sofa so that the dog does not climb on it.

• Elevate the bin so that the dog does not access it.

These preventive measures will allow you to be focused entirely on the exercises to be taught.

A Good Dog: The Key to Proper Training

The excellent training of the dog is a promise of well-being and serenity, both for you (the practice of cleanliness in the puppy must be the first step of training, for example); and for him. To be fully receptive to practice, your dog must be physically and mentally fit. He must be fed appropriately according to his needs. He must drink enough water.

It will help if you also respect its essential rest times and adapt to its condition, its age, etc. A puppy, for example, sleeps a lot, sometimes up to 90% of his time. He will learn quickly, but you have to prepare short training sessions! Preferably to take place before meals, but without starving it. Using one of your small dog kibbles will be an excellent way to get his attention during the training session: he must, therefore, have an appetite, but not get impatient.

A Good Dog: The Key to Proper Training

Your dog needs to be entertained, so spend time with him to play, to go out, to make him meet other dogs

Make him play sports; he also needs to drain his energy!

In conclusion, take care of the complete development of your dog; its training will only be more productive.

CHAPTER THREE

How to Make Your Four-Legged Friend Understand Your Body Language

Being understood by your dog is not easy. Man and animals do not speak the same language, and communication cannot be established naturally without adopting the right gestures. However, talking to your dog is essential to build a relationship of trust and to learn to understand each other. The animal gradually decrypts your intention through your words, gestures, and intonations of voice. It's up to you to learn to be clear, concise, gentle, consistent and above all, very patient. Discover the best practices to make your animal understand by speaking.

Oral language is a great way to communicate with humans, but also with your dog. Animals communicate much more with their bodies, but they perceive the message through your voice.

By communicating with his animal every day, the master teaches him to understand; the dog gets used to it and learns to follow you through your intonations, your words, your types of sentences and it can associate your body behavior and your facial expressions with being sure to decipher the message. The same goes for the master who seeks to understand his dog according to his barking, the movements of his tail, or the position of his ears, for example. It's an original, unique language that develops between the animal and its owner over time.

How to Address Your Animal

To be clearly understood, you must not talk to your animal in just any way. First, grab his attention by calling him by name and looking at him. This is how he understands that you have something to say to him. If he's staring at you carefully, he's ready to listen to you.

Don't be surprised if your pet doesn't understand you at the start of your relationship. You don't speak the same language. Be patient, and above all, be very forgiving; human language is not written in the dog's genes, it can be learned. Guide your animal in its learning by playing on the intonations and your body attitude. These are, above all, the sounds and intonations that the dog perceives and interprets.

Over time, your pet will understand what you have to say. He will know that "no" is forbidden, that "stroll" or "walk" means that you are going to go out, or that "eat" or "bowl" is synonymous with a meal. You will then see that your pet is listening to you, that he is going to get his leash for the walk, that he is waiting for you at the door, or even in front of his bowl. For the dog, speaking is also a synonym of confidence; speak to him, and he will be happy to learn how to please you and be useful to you.

Talking to Your Dog: How to Be Understood

Being understood by your dog is not easy and requires patience. Do not imagine that your pet will understand you effortlessly. For a relationship to be established and dialogue to take place, it is imperative to adopt the right methods to make yourself heard.

• Be concise

Do not use long sentences when talking to your dog; he will not understand you. It is essential to be brief and get straight to the point, both in words and intonation. The same goes for its name; if it is too long and complicated, it will have more difficulty recognizing it.

When you talk to him, be efficient, but not aggressive. It is not useful to give an order in a dry and authoritarian tone. Speak gently to your pet to make you understand better: "come," "sit," "calm," "go get it," "are you playing?" etc. On the other hand, if he is disobedient, say "no" firmly, but without violence. A threatening index may be enough to make him obey or to point out that he did wrong.

• Be gentle and patient

Softness and patience are essential in the context of your relationship with your animal, but also dialogue! If you are kind, your pet will trust you and act well. If he does something stupid, there is no point in yelling at him because he will perceive you as an attacker; speak to him as to a child who would have misbehaved, with gentleness and diplomacy. Your pet sees your intention in your intonations; thus, if you are aggressive, it will distance itself from you and may perceive your aggression as an injustice.

• Be consistent in your orders

When speaking to it, try always to use the same language. Your dog will understand you much better with a short and precise prescription, which uses the same words. If you diversify your vocabulary too much to express a single order, you risk disturbing it, and it will not be able to perceive your intention. Choose a word for each order and make sure everyone in the family sticks to it.

• Use your body

To help your dog understand you, talk with body movements. Your animal must quickly identify your intention, also thanks to your gestures. The raised finger can be a "no"; the caress can be a reward, etc. Associate a gesture with each order to make yourself understood and primarily to facilitate the learning of your dog.

• Think about contact

Contact is essential in your relationship and your communication with your animal. Pet your dog, scratch it, touch it to build confidence. You show him that you are available to him. The sides, chest, and belly are privileged places to express your friendship. On the other hand, the head is a place of submission, so caress it kindly.

How Should You Punish a Puppy or Dog Justly When He Does Something Stupid?

Your dog may do some stupid things, and you don't know how to make him understand that this is not what you want. How should you "correct" your dog: is it useful? How can the punishment be effective, fair, and consistent?

First of all, it is important to understand how the dog learns to know how to teach him which behavior is okay and which behavior is not.

The dog learns by operative conditioning. That is, if a payment follows an action, it repeats it. On the other hand, if an effort leads to a sanction (something unpleasant for the dog), he will try to avoid this behavior.

The goal of learning is not to keep the dog always in avoidance! No, on the contrary, the goal is that he understands what attitude allows him to obtain satisfaction.

How to Discipline Your Dog: The Ideal Scheme

To do this, it is essential that the punishments are not traumatic for the dog, that they are simply fair and consistent for him. And for this to be the case, it is essential always to follow a punishment with a reward so that the following association is clear for your dog:

To understand this, here is the diagram to follow when you want to punish your dog for bad behavior:

• Punishment

The discipline should not be violent; it must be fair and consistent based on your dog's bad behavior. Never hit your dog; it would only cause your dog to fear you and no longer trust you.

Talking to Your Dog: How to Be Understood?

Being understood by your dog is not easy and requires patience. Do not imagine that your pet will understand you effortlessly. For a relationship to be established and dialogue to take place, it is imperative to adopt the right methods to make yourself heard.

Be concise

Do not make long sentences when talking to your dog; he will not understand you. It is essential to be brief and get straight to the point, both in words and intonation.

The same goes for its name; if it is too long and complicated, it will have more difficulty recognizing it.

When you talk to him, be efficient, but not aggressive. It is not useful to give an order in a dry and authoritarian tone. Speak gently to your pet to make you understand better: "come," "sit," "calm," "go get it," "are you playing?", etc. On the other hand, if he is disobedient, say "no" firmly, but without violence. A threatening finger may be enough to make him obey or to point out that he did wrong.

CHAPTER FOUR

Understanding Your Four-Legged Friend's Body Language

Your four-legged friend has no spoken language to communicate stress to you. He uses body language made up of a variety of signals that are often referred to as "calming signals." Discover ten signs of discomfort in dogs to understand their emotional state better.

Dogs can understand a wide range of emotions, including stress and discomfort. They usually express them through their body language, commonly known as "calming signals". These signals are used to warn a human or fellow that the dog is experiencing discomfort or stress, but they also serve to help the dog calm down. There are, therefore, several behaviors and attitudes that your dog will show to indicate feelings of discomfort and stress.

Understanding your dog's emotional state is essential to alleviating unwanted symptoms and helping your dog feel comfortable. Then, respecting this state in the dog means removing it from the situation that makes it uncomfortable or reassuring him. Unfortunately, many are unable to "hear" what their dog is trying to tell them. To help you better understand your canine companion, here are ten signs of discomfort to be aware of in dogs.

1.The diversion of the gaze or head

This behavior is used to demonstrate that the dog is not threatening and that he does not want conflict. The dog can also turn his head to indicate that he is stressed and needs a break.

We humans can just as well turn our heads to get the same message to the dog. Dogs understand very well the appeasement signals given by humans.

2. Yawning

A dog that does not feel comfortable in a given situation will often express it by excessive yawning when it is not tired. Yawning can then lead to vocalization, such as barking, moaning, or grunting.

Since dogs do not usually express their discomfort with a single calming signal, observe if your doggie also exhibits other typical behavior to confirm its trouble.

3. Licking the muzzle

Another sign that your dog is stressed is licking the muzzle repeatedly. Dogs lick their noses to appease a person or animal they perceive as a threat to ward off aggression. An example of this can be found in the dog who is reprimanded when his humans, after being away all day, come home to find out that he had an "accident" in the house. You could then notice that the dog looks away and licks his muzzle repeatedly.

4. Sniffing the ground

Does your dog suddenly sniff the ground in the presence of other dogs or humans? Or does he live in the countryside and find himself in a noisy urban environment? He may try to calm his stress by finding himself in a situation that he does not necessarily like. In this way, it also indicates to others around it that it needs space.

5. Bypass

Have you ever noticed that dogs usually approach sideways and rarely face to face? The bypass and the slow approach are strong signs of appeasement that express a peaceful approach (I don't want any conflict). You could say it's a sign of politeness in dogs.

Indeed, launching directly on another dog is not very polite, it is as if a stranger would throw himself on you to give you a hug. I'm not sure you would appreciate it!

6. Shake

Is your dog completely dry and shaking vigorously? He uses an effective method to relieve his stress. For example, when you physically force him (like the vet) and put him back on the ground, chances are he will shake himself to get over his stress and calm down.

Another example: if you have just taught your dog a new trick, he may shake himself to ventilate all the intellectual work he has just provided.

7. Humping

It's a generally ignored sign of appeasement. The overlap is not necessarily sexual. Some stressed dogs adopt this strategy to calm down. I agree that it doesn't necessarily appease the other dog or human! However, be aware that this behavior may indicate some stress and discomfort in your dog.

8. Panting

A dog who feels great discomfort, pain or is very stressed will pant intensely and quickly. Also, just like us, his respiratory rate and his muscular tension increase in times of high stress.

9. Excessively salivating and sweating

It is common for dogs that stressed people produce more saliva than usual, even in the absence of hot temperatures or recent exercise. And just like their humans, dogs placed in a stressful environment also experience a rise in their body temperature, which causes sweating around the nose and pads.

10. Adopting a "low" posture

If your dog is troubled with a situation, or if he is afraid, watch his body language, especially his general attitude, as well as the position of his tail and ears.

The fearful and stressed dog will take a rounded position, will tuck its tail between its hind legs, and its ears will tend to move back on the head while flattening. It will make you feel like you want to disappear or blend in with the background and will try to flee if it gets the chance.

What to Do When Your Dog Is Stressed?

Is your dog sending you clear signals of discomfort? The best thing you can do for him, if possible, is to keep him away from the situation that makes him uncomfortable. You can also get him used to make the stressful situation more reassuring for him.

The relationship between a dog and its human should always be based on respect, and your best friend counts on you to protect him from what scares him. Be attentive and proactive if you notice signs of discomfort in your dog. And if your dog's fears prevent him from enjoying life to the full, never hesitate to consult a competent and up-to-date dog trainer.

Cohabitation Between Dogs

There are different types of cohabitation between dogs that will have an impact on the atmosphere in your home:

- Cohabitation between males

- Cohabitation between females
- Male and female cohabitation
- Cohabitation between adult dogs and a puppy

The type that is generally the least easy to manage is cohabitation between males. Indeed, it seems that the males are more territorial than the fair sex if there are numbers of them then definitely you are going to have conflicts. It can also occur between various types of cohabitation.

Also, with proper supervision or with the help of advice from a dog trainer, cohabitation between males can be a positive experience.

That said, it is generally easier to have a male and a female cohabitate than several males together. If you don't want the female to reproduce, you have to make sure that the animals are operated, of course.

After that, the well-socialized adult dog can serve as a model for the puppy and teach him good canine manners and contributing to his good socialization.

Regardless of the type of cohabitation, care must be taken to ensure that dogs have sufficient space, exercise, and training to increase the chances that cohabitation will go well. And most importantly, remember that the rules that apply to one of your dogs also apply to the others.

How to Manage the First Meeting

Here are some rules to increase the chances that the first meeting between two dogs that will cohabit will go well:

- Choose a neutral place, preferably outside
- Take a long walk with the two dogs, being at the start, at a great distance from each other, to better get closer gradually without letting the dogs touch each other.
- Take into account the signs of appeasement and stress in your dogs
- Repeat the experience of parallel walks several times over short periods (less than 15 minutes).
- Reward dogs during a parallel walk with delicacies (cheese, beef liver, boiled chicken, etc.)

After more than five meetings and side-by-side walks that went well, you can try to let the dogs smell. If the dogs seem under stress, you can let them go free in a neutral place by making reminders every minute (which has the function of reducing tensions between the two dogs, if there are any).

Remind the two dogs of yours as often as possible (even if there is no argument) and give them rewards. This will force the two dogs to take breaks from their game, as well as to have positive experiences together.

Some owners are tempted to take a second dog with the hope that this will solve the dog's behavioral problems they already have (e.g., separation anxiety, barking, etc.).

On the contrary, you simply risk having several dogs dealing with behavioral problems.

CHAPTER FIVE

New Puppy Survival Guide

You've taken the plunge: you've added a new member to your family. And even more so, since you have chosen a puppy! This beautiful little ball of irresistible fur has conquered your eyes and your heart. The first emotions are sweet, and you are in love with your little one promised.

Note, however, that waking up after the "honeymoon" can be difficult. The reality and the surprises of the first days can desecrate the ideas you had in mind.

To avoid unnecessary disappointment, here is a list of things to expect when you welcome a puppy into your life:

Your New Puppy May Experience Stress

A puppy or an adult dog are individuals made in the same way as a human being; they have habits and benchmarks. Your puppy will have the same reaction to change; it will feel stress. Put yourself in his shoes and imagine for a minute that someone comes to withdraw you from your house to make you live with strangers in a whole new environment. You might be out of phase, right? The same goes for your puppy. Under his cheerful and innocent looks, mini-Fido saw a big upheaval. And stress can lead to several things such as refusal to eat, lack of stools, diarrhea, crying, etc.

The first thing is that they do not panic. Your puppy will gradually take its cues. The best you can do to help it is to keep your good habits and also to:

• Make him explore your environment with a treat for each new room discovered

• Give him the food he is used to avoiding further change and the risk of diarrhea.

• If you have to change the type of food, proceed very gradually, mixing the two types over several days. And even before making the change, wait at least one or two weeks for your puppy to be a little more used to your home.

• Give him food to help the digestive system in case of diarrhea (you can find it at your veterinarian)

• Show him where his things are: the sleeping cushion, the bowls for eating and drinking, your bedroom, his training cage, the outside courtyard where he can do his business.

The First Night With Your Puppy

You guessed it: the first night can be difficult, a bit like with a new baby. Your puppy will probably be afraid of being in the dark or alone in an unknown house. He may then cry, scratch, or scratch. Not to mention its natural needs that will have to be met. In fact, your puppy will still be unable to hold back all night. We offer you some useful ways to adopt during this night time period:

• Preferably, install his cage in your room and near you: this has the advantage of comforting your puppy with your presence and also of allowing you to be nearby if you need to reassure him.

• At first, you will not know why your dog is crying: does he need to pee? Does he feel alone? Is he hungry? To start potty training right away, make yourself available, and get the puppy out if you hear it crying. But be careful, to avoid your baby thinking that a play period is coming, take him out calmly: do not talk to him, go out with him without saying anything and do not spend more than 5 minutes outside with him. If he peed or poop, well done! Reward him with a little treat and then go home. If he did nothing, come back in again and put it back in its cage calmly. It will be for next time!

• Do not hesitate to reassure your puppy if you think he is stressed: speak to him in a soft and low voice, extend his hand to him so that he can smell your smell.

The First Walk With Your Dog

In general, the first walks of a puppy are chaotic! Fido does not know where to go, he does not know what you expect from him, everything smells good, and everything must be explored at the same time, the noises can be stressful, the leash looks more like a chew toy, etc. So, how can you make the first outing pleasant?

• Above all, bring the right equipment: a suitable harness (if possible with a tie at the front, this will help you manage your draft dog side), a flat collar equipped with its medal, several poo bags, treats.

• Choose a short course; the puppies are not used to walking; it is better to go out several times if necessary and avoid long strenuous walks. You might make him see walks in a negative way.

• Also, consider taking breaks from play during the walk or even "odor" breaks. Your puppy needs to discover the world around him, and he will do it with his nose, just like you do with your eyes.

• If your puppy is dragging its paw to finish the course, go into play mode, and encourage it to follow you running. Your dog should follow you more cheerfully. Reward him with a treat.

The First Contact With Other Animals

This point is crucial: your puppy will start socializing. His first contacts will later define how he will associate and apprehend the presence of other animals around him.

• To avoid problems, avoid leash contact during walks. Indeed, many dogs are reactive, and most of the time, contact on a leash generates a lot of frustration on both sides.

• If necessary, call a friend who has a well-rounded adult puppy or dog to walk with you or to organize play periods with your dog. Our dog education Facebook group could help you find people near you to play with.

• With other animals in the house, for example, a cat, be sure to present it on a leash, that the cat has a place to flee in case of fear and teach your dog to come back to you and look at you. This situation.

The First Time You Leave Your Puppy Alone

When you choose to have a puppy, it's best to make sure you have time for it. If the whole family is away for the whole day, and it is impossible to do otherwise, I can only advise you against having a baby dog. You have to be there period.

That said, your puppy will have to be alone even if you are regularly present with him. So how do you do it?

• Make sure from the start of his arrival that you have trained him well in his cage. Does he enter it willingly? Does he still hesitate? How much?

• Can he stay alone without crying? Adjust your first outing based on your answers.

• Make it short. Avoid ending up in an emergency that will make you leave the premises for more than 2 hours the first time. Start with a small hour-long outing. The best thing is to get used to it gradually before: 5 minutes, then 10, then 20, then 45, etc.

• Make him do his business before leaving.

• Invite him to enter his cage, offer him new toys to chew on. Give him a treat or two when he's in it and then close the door.

• When you come back, don't rush to him excited and worried about how things have been. Avoid the emotions associated with departures and returns. Your puppy must feel that everything is normal when you leave, and when you return: put down your coat, put down your things. Wait for your four-legged friend to calm down before coming to open it.

Take the essential, a kindergarten class with your puppy! Indeed, a good kindergarten class will allow you to learn much more than the basics of obedience to your doggie. Inhibition of bite, management of jumps and nibbles, walking, recall, games between puppies supervised under the watchful eye of canine trainers will be concepts to which you will have access.

How to Eradicate Your Puppy's Nibbles and Jumps!

Is your puppy jumping? Is your puppy chewing? Good news! You have a normal and healthy puppy! You might as well put it into perspective! However, these behaviors can be unpleasant, and many tips are available on the internet and in books to stop these behaviors. So how do you get there, and most importantly, have a method that works?

First, it must be understood that very often, puppies bite or jump on you to get attention! Talk to them, push them away, or shout wind to excite your puppy further! Is this really what you want?

Second, it's okay to get mad at your puppy if it hurts you, or worse yet, knocks your kids down! However, avoid falling into the trap and punishing your puppy by scaring or hurting him! For example, never do the following:

- Tap it on the muzzle

- Hold its mouth

- Take it by the neck and shake it

Unfortunately, many of the clients I have had have made their puppy aggressive or fearful of body manipulation using such training methods.

What Do You Do With The Puppy that Jumps?

Ignore the puppy that jumps, and tell him absolutely nothing.

Your puppy wants your attention! Giving it to him will make him want to jump on you again! Don't push him away; don't tell him no. Show him that he doesn't exist when he's not behaving well. My chapter on how to decrease your dog's unacceptable behavior could also help you.

However, why do you always have to react to a bad behavior? The best is to note the contexts that make your puppy jump and to teach him a more acceptable behavior ... For example, sit calmly.

The Contexts that Make the Puppy Jump:

Does your puppy tend to jump when you serve him a bowl of food? Does he tend to jump when you get home? When he gets out of his cage? When are you handling objects, and he has no access to them? Practice a sit down as well as self-control exercises in these contexts!

Here, you use the set command, which you already taught Dali outside of training sessions to better control the jumps and excitement related to putting on his leash:

Here, Fido must sit down to receive his meal! What if your puppy gets excited when you lower the bowl to the ground? Raise it and repeat the exercise until your puppy is calm!

Here you are waiting for Fido to sit down to get her out of the cage. When she is allowed out, the coach says, "Okay!"

• Using rewards, teach your new dog to look at you.

• Punish the puppy by removing it (or by withdrawing):

When your puppy jumps on you, it is because he wants attention. Show him that jumping is an entirely ineffective way to get it! This punishment is not intended to scare or hurt your puppy. Its purpose is to take away what he desires when he engages in behavior that is deemed unacceptable. A bit like with a child who is "deprived" of the right to watch television since he has raised his voice towards his parents!

The scenario:

1. Your dog jumps on you

2. You say "Too bad" as soon as it jumps on you

3. Then you bring it in its cage, put it in another room or you withdraw yourself in another room

4. You start again as long as your puppy begins again! It is essential to be consistent!

Pro Tip: Leave a small leash on your puppy at all times! Short enough not to get caught in furniture, long enough for you to grab or step on while your puppy is standing.

Then, when your puppy nibbles or jumps on you, it will not be able to have more fun because you take it by the collar to lead to his cage or in the punishment room. Also, if he jumps on you, you can put your foot on the leash so you can ignore it brilliantly!

It is essential when you decide to punish your dog (by removing a privilege) to be consistent! If you punish him once for X behavior, you must do it each time he produces said behavior. Otherwise, he will not be able to link his behavior and the consequence because the consequence is too variable.

It is normal for your puppy, the first few times, to test a lot by continuing to jump despite the punishments. Usually, twenty repetitions are necessary the first time before the puppy stops the behavior that you want to see decrease! Thereafter, the puppy calms down more and more quickly.

Example of Effective Punishments for a Puppy that Bites or Jumps:

1. Go into another room for 30 seconds.

2. Put him in a place where there is nothing to do (for example the bathroom) for 30 seconds

3. If your puppy likes his crate, using it occasionally as a place to pick up can also be a good option. Make sure the cage is empty and boring, however.

What to Do With the Puppy that Nibbles?

It is time to teach your little shark what to bite ... Or not! First, giving exciting activities to your puppy will do a lot to make you "less interesting" to bother—jumps and nibbles included! It doesn't matter how small Fido is; he is very energetic, and he needs exciting toys to chew on.

Ideas to occupy the puppy that bites:

1. A pulling rope dipped in chicken broth then frozen

2. Make him a "Popsicle" for a dog with a plastic bowl filled with water, a handle of kibble and a little chicken broth

3. Give him all his meals in interactive toys

4. Buy him all kinds of chewing bones

5. Understand the puppy's nibbles

There are two types of biting in puppies:

1. To play

2. To demonstrate discomfort

How to tell the difference? When the puppy nibbles to "play", it comes to you! When it nibbles because it is uncomfortable, it happens in a context where you handle it. For example, you take him in your arms, and he bites your hands. It's not a game! As for the puppy that nips because it does not like to be handled, you see all the handling procedures in our kindergarten puppy lesson online. With the puppy coming towards you and nibbling at us, you assume that it does so because it wants your attention or because it wants to play!

Here is the procedure for this kind of puppy:

• If he does not bite hard (that is, he does not put a lot of pressure, that it does not create pain), you can redirect your puppy to his favorite toy.

• If he chews hard (you feel enormous pressure, a lack of control, a pinch), you say

"Too bad," and then you withdraw (or you withdraw) for a few seconds.

Bite Inhibition, Important Training!

The primary purpose of all these training sessions is to prohibit all nibbling! The goal is to make your puppy understand that his mouth has a certain strength and that he must learn to control it! So, later, if it comes to bite, it will be able to control its mouth and will not create significant damage! One of the vigorous exercise you can have to teach your puppy!

Good news, the nibbles "to play" disappear by themselves over time in more than 95% in this case, without any training! However, around 4 and 5 months, when your puppy loses his puppy teeth and his adult teeth grow, he will start chewing again! Do not worry, it's normal.

It doesn't convey that your puppy is a monster or that it "regresses" or that it tests you! Giving her lots of bones and frozen toys will go a long way in helping you get through these difficult weeks.

I also suggest that you play "pull a toy" with your puppy, which will teach him exactly the difference between a toy and your hands, in addition, to be a great exercise in self-control and a return to calm.

Here I have a chapter to show you how to do it, and above all, how to do it right:

Inhibiting the bite is important!

Take advantage of this period in your puppy's life to teach him to control the strength of his bite! It will be his best life insurance! Why? Because if one day he comes to bite a dog or a human (for example, if he is afraid or upset), he will know how to control his mouth and avoid doing major damage. Do not think that your puppy will never bite! Because everything with teeth can bite! Even you!

The puppy that jumps and nibbles ... Nothing is more normal!But I know very, very well that these behaviors are most frustrating and sometimes painful.

However, be patient and remember the key concepts:

1. Don't scare or hurt your puppy

2. Show her what to chew on

3. Give him something to take care of

4. Show her what to do instead of jumping

5. Using withdrawal as a punishment

I hope I could help you with your little hybrid between a piranha and a tornado!

The Importance of Socialization In Puppies

This section is about developing social relationships, adapting, and integrating into social life. In the end, your puppy learns to be a dog. But, above all, it learns to be an emotionally healthy dog, which will evolve in complete stability in its human environment.

In a canine context, the puppy will learn not to have a negative emotional reaction when faced with everyday situations:

• Various manipulations: getting your claws cut, getting your ears touched, brushing your teeth, etc.

• Different environments depending on the case: parks, dog parks, busy streets, lakes, forests, schools, hospitals, workplaces, etc.

• Different humans: young, elderly, toddlers, people of different colors, different physical aspects, different approaches, etc.

• Different animals with which it will be in contact: horse, rodent, cat, bird, etc.

- Teach him to get into the car

- Communicating with peers, "talking to the dog"

- To share things without conflict

- To inhibit its bite

Puppy Brain Development

Brain organization begins at the age of 5 to 7 weeks. It consists, in parallel with this cell multiplication, in the destruction of unnecessary cells and contacts. This "suicide" phase ends around the age of 3 to 4 months.

Work actually starts from the first day: Adopting your furball. The first five months are very crucial. Thereafter, he returned to adulthood; it will be necessary to maintain his social gains by continuing to expose him to different stimuli situations. It is advisable to register for a socialization course if you feel uninformed or helpless about the behavior of your pet.

Pros of Socialization In Pets.

By integrating a living being into its environment, it can live in harmony with it. This will prevent your dog from developing certain behavioral problems:

- Phobias

- Aggression

- Deprivation syndrome

- "Hyper" behavior, anxiety and stress

One of the greatest positive aspects of socialization that begins early and is well conducted in the absence of predation towards the species that your animal will encounter in everyday life. Indeed, it is possible that Fido dreams of tasting cats if he did not learn that they are a "friendly" and not "edible" species during his early childhood. Socialization is the only way to guarantee that the dog will not have predatory behavior towards "friendly" species.

Get him used to see humans of all colors, of both sexes, of all ages and ... in all positions! A human is not the same shape standing, crouching, or walking on all fours!

So, in the case of a "grasshopper puppy," you will teach him that jumping on passers-by is never a rewarding attitude while sitting wisely always earns him an attention mark or a kibble!

Behavioral Training or Infectious Prevention?

The debate between the risks of disease versus socialization is still much talked about…

Even if you don't take your puppy out, it is not immune to viruses because you bring it back every day through your shoes and clothes. What's necessary to understand is that the period of socialization of a puppy only lasts a time: up to 4 months, in general.

During this period, it is easy to present new stimuli, new situations, and new beings to him, which will be associated with positive moments. It is also during this period that he will learn to recognize the "friendly" species, the one that would not hunt him, and the ones that he should not hunt. Unfortunately, most behavioral problems are linked to poor socialization.

The best thing is to take your puppy out as much as possible (and even give him the benefit of education lessons) while preventing him from being in contact with the droppings of other animals.

Teaching Puppy Cleanliness

During the first two months of its existence, much like in a young child, it is completely normal for your puppy to be unable to hold back. Later, the young dog will get into the habit of going to the bathroom away from the places where he is used to sleeping and eating. As for the rest, it is the duty of each owner to teach his dog the appropriate place where he can relieve himself.

Whether your dog is two months or eight years old, the way to teach him about cleanliness remains the same: You must physically restrict your dog when you cannot supervise him, take him out as often as possible, and effectively clean all traces of odors.

The key to success will be prevention, which is to keep your dog from practicing poaching somewhere other than the agreed location.

Using the Cage to Teach Your Dog Cleanliness

The best way to prevent Fido from dirtying the floor when you can't watch it is by caging it.

If you are reluctant to put your companion in such a confinement, it would probably be useful to read the following chapter: How to leave my dog in his crate comfortably?

The bottom line is that when a cage is used properly, it becomes a reassuring little house for your companion if it is not a place of punishment and synonymous with "dog jail."

The proof? A dog who has been gradually and gently taught to love the cage will go to rest there on its own when the door is opened. Mentally and physically stimulate your puppy/dog so that he can use his crate as a resting place.

The Ideal Size for Your Dog's Cage

Since your companion has an instinctive habit of not defiling the place where he rests, a place to rest is of supreme importance. Ideally, the area you should provide for your dog should be enough so that he can be comfortable lying down so that he can get up and so that he can change place.

To make your dog learn how to restrain himself quickly, it is important that he cannot relieve himself in one dark and suffocated area of his cage and then sleep in another one.

Usually, cages have the arrangement to divide, and they are available in the market, which will come in handy. Your dog will learn to hold back, and, little by little, you will be able to offer him more space!

Carefully Watch Your Puppy

Aim for prevention rather than punishment! Learn more about the different methods of dog training: punish or prevent?

When you catch him, stay calm, take him outside immediately, and reward if he finishes his needs outside. Always bringing him to the same place to relieve himself will help him to train potty because he will smell his smell there.

If he does not make his needs when you take him outside of your home, you must put him back in his cage or use a leash that you will hang on your waist to prevent him from finding a quiet place where he can do its needs.

Whichever method you choose, take your dog out again in the next few minutes.

• If he does his business, then give him a treat

• Carry on your practice he is not picking up and repeats it until he eliminates outside

• Don't forget to give him a treat.

If you apply this methodology, then your partner will know how to go outside with his needs.

Properly Clean Soiled Surfaces

Too often, customers who consult me confess that they have used various cleaning items like bleach, etc. These items have ammonia and contain a certain level of pH and force your dog to use the toilet in the same place by reinforcing the natural smell of his excrement.

So the best advice is to utilize vinegar instead of bleach and, along with vinegar, use water to clean up the mess.

Your Dog Urinates in the House: Behavioral Causes to Consider

Your dog may be desperate. Excretion allows him to pass out some of the stress. No need to punish your dog, otherwise his housekeeping problems will get worse.

When it comes to emotional peeing, staying unaware of the dog's behavior is very important and also ask your dog to do so until it is calm enough to be flattered without being overly excited.

If necessary, you can consult a dog trainer or a canine behavior expert who will be able to precisely assess your needs.

Does Your Dog Have a Health Problem?

Perhaps the reason that your pet relieves himself in the house is and, unfortunately, medical. Here is a shortlist of the evils that could affect your dog:

- Urinary tract infection

- Incontinence related to aging

- Diabetes

- Kidney disease

Do you think your pet is suffering from one of these illnesses? Contact your veterinarian now!

A Clean Dog in a Few Easy Steps

To make your dog understand where his needs should be relieved, remember to use the following method:

1. Use the crate to restrain your dog when he is not in sight

2. Take your animal out as often as possible and reward it

3. Remove all traces of urine and droppings.

4. Never punish your dog in accidents

Finally, if this can help you stay calm during Fido accidents, keep in mind that it took you two or even three years before acquiring cleanliness!

If you feel that you are not able to be disciplined, organized, or available enough to teach your dog and hire a competent dog walker who can get your furball out as often as possible.

Five Stubborn Myths About Exercise In Puppies

You have a new puppy. All-new, all beautiful! Like any good new parent of a furry ball, you are determined to do things the best you can. Now, your puppy has barely arrived home when the contradictory advice on his health and safety is pouring in.

Between your dog training readings that explain that an exhausted dog is a dog that is not a nuisance, your friends' recommendations to limit exercise and alarmist publications on social networks about the dangers of ball games, sticks, babiche bones or marrow bones you no longer know who to believe or what to do.

Where is the safe balance between calculating each walk to the minute, and meeting your puppy's physical activity needs to ensure that he is calm? In short, how to preserve the long-term health of your new friend without ending up with a monster that destroys your living room or a puppy that nibbles everything in its path? Let's clear this up by dissecting some myths about puppies and exercise frequently heard by dog trainers!

"A puppy must not do exercise above five minutes of physical activity per month of age in a day."

The rule of five minutes maximum exercise per month of puppy age per day is a good scale in order to gauge the exercise imposed continuously properly.

In order to avoid repetitive movements, it is usually recommended to do five minutes per month of the prescribed exercise age. i.e., you have a toddler two months pet; then, he is entitled to 10 minutes of compulsory exercise. If he's three months old, he's entitled to a whopping 15 minutes!

Examples of exercises that can be practiced continuously:

• Playing with the ball (gently rolling the ball)

• Walking on a leash

• Playing tug-of-war

• Running (avoid with a dog under 12 months old)

• Recall practices

It is important to limit these activities. During these activities, your puppy is not free to change its rhythm or do something else.

When it comes to free-ranging exercises like exploring, playing in the garden with your puppy, or with another dog, or leaving it free, there is no limit. Your puppy is free to stop, go to bed if tired, get up, and change hobbies! During these activities, your puppy is free to change its rhythm or do something else.

Very physically demanding activities such as ball games, running, or jumping are to be avoided in a puppy.

Note: Avoid doing long, continuous exercise sessions with your puppy. Try to divide your 15-minute session (for a three-month-old puppy) into several small sessions.

If your puppy is hyperactive and energetic, that might be because you haven't exhausted him enough. Our dogs lack physical exercise, and this is often what creates many behavioral problems. If it is necessary to move your puppy for good mental and physical health and good development, however, you must be careful not to make him do too much.

Does the Energetic Puppy Still Lack Exercise?

An energetic puppy is not always a puppy that needs exercise. A puppy whose energy is boosted on the return from walking is not necessarily because the activity was too short ... But maybe because it was too long! Young puppies and adolescent dogs can quickly become over-stimulated. A stimulated puppy will become frantic, be unable to lie down and be quiet, jump on you, or turn your living room into a running track.

To avoid these situations, take a test: do shorter activities with little Fido and watch his energy level when you get home. Is he calmer? If the answer is yes, it is that the walks were too long and had the effect of making him over-excited!

Other puppies may need help learning to be calm. Certain breeds such as the Malinois, German Shepherd, Border Collie or other high energy dogs do not know, when they are young, how to stay calm. Show your new friend that staying quiet and sleeping is a good activity by giving them a reward when they sleep on their pillow.

So how do I exercise my puppy?

1. Mentally stimulate him

2. Give him all his meals in interactive toys

3. Teach your puppy tricks

4. Practice low-impact dog sports such as odor detection or

Dog Fitness Myths

• "My puppy must have had a long sleep last night. "

Using only physical activity to keep your puppy busy can have long-term negative effects on his health and behavior. This is a persistent myth that can prove to be dangerous. In order to properly burn the energy of your puppy, you go outside with a ball; you go for an hour ride, or even you run to drain your battery.

These redundant movement activities can injure your puppy and cause permanent damage. Many dog owners think that their dog needs five miles of running a day to be happy and to sleep. On the contrary, only relying on physical activity to exhaust a puppy is not only dangerous but will also create endurance; your puppy will always need longer and longer outings to be calm.

Rather than taking little Fido outside for a walk because he's bored, give him a bone to chew on or do a short, fun clicker workout to exhaust him mentally.

Give him all of his meals in interactive toys so that he spends a good part of his day eating and eating, just like in the wild. All of these tactics will allow you to keep your new companion exhausted, happy to have worked! Also, they will avoid long-term health problems.

• "Do Not Allow Your Puppy to Go Downstairs"

Ah, the steps and the stairs! Many people have heard that a dog should never go up or down the steps before the age of one. Indeed, going up and down the steps is a repetitive physical activity that can create long-term problems in the joints.

A lot of studies have inferred the results that the onset of hip dysplasia increases when puppies less than three months old go up and down stairs several times a day. Although these results were only demonstrated on breeds with high chances of developing this disease; the consensus in all breeds is to avoid puppies going up and down stairs repeatedly before the end of their growth.

However, it is also during the growth period that your dog acquires the motor skills necessary to make the movements that it will be called upon to produce as an adult. If your dog has never learned to go up and down the steps, it is very likely that as he gets older, he has fears or difficulties with the stairs. The key here is moderation. You especially don't want to be caught for the next ten years with a Dane who is afraid to go down the stairs!

Of course, don't play a ball game on the steps. Petit Fido can, however, occasionally go up and down two or three steps. Excess, in one direction as much as in the other, is to be avoided!

• "You cannot start any dog sports with your dog for a year."

As you have said many times, repetitive physical activity and puppies do not mix well.

However, in the majority of canine sports, there are foundation exercises to do with little Fido. Many of these exercises can be started as soon as your puppy arrives home and are safe for your protection.

In addition to giving you ideas for mentally stimulating activities for your new treasure, learning foundation exercises will weld your team together and allow your dog to have a solid knowledge base when he is fully grown!

Some ideas for foundation exercises:

- Teach your dog to look at you
- Teach your dog the principle of the clicker
- Teach him the basic commands
- Teach your puppy to like to put on his harness (very useful if you plan to practice canicross!)
- Teach him the directions in canicross (without traction)
- Teach your puppy to love putting his paws on different surfaces
- Teach your puppy that you exist despite distractions
- Teach your puppy about self-checks
- Teach your puppy to follow the tension on the leash

And much more!

What Should You Do With a Puppy that Barks at Night?

Some think hearing a rooster crowing before daybreak is frustrating. And yet, contrary to popular belief, it does happen at other times as well. A rooster will sing if he feels a danger near the chicken coop, such as a roaming animal or an unusual light. The animals are similar, and their survival instincts are powerful.

Even if your dogs are domesticated to adapt to human life, it is the same for them: they have instincts and reflexes that make them bark or cry in certain situations. The night period is no exception to the rule. While most of us humans sleep deeply, for dogs, this is not always the case.

Let's see together what are some of the situations where our pets decide to play the raging owls and what are the solutions to help them not do it anymore—and let you sleep!

1. The dog barks after hearing outside noise

A passerby who walks, the neighbor's barking dog, and a raccoon who searches the trash cans are all night microphenomena that can pollute your dog's tranquility and make him react. After all, it's their role: to protect their home and land from potential harm. He does not know that the passer-by is harmless or that the raccoon will be satisfied by a few pieces of trash before leaving for his burrow.

So it warns you that something is going on and tries to scare the intruder away.

"Well done, my dog! Good job! Well ... you could have refrained from doing it at 3am for a mosquito anyway ... "

The best thing to do to prevent your dog from being afraid of surrounding noise is to keep it in your room overnight. This will make him less likely to hear outside sounds, and you will be there to reassure him if something happens.

Other solutions to reduce your dog's barking at night:

• Put your dog in the quietest room of the house, away from the noise.

• Use white noise to mask other ambient noise, for example, a fan or soft music.

• Using a crate at night for your dog, if it is well integrated, has a calming effect on many canines and tends to reassure them

2. The dog barks because he is anxious

Sometimes dogs can react very severely to the separation from their owner or their family and suffer from separation anxiety. Bedtime, therefore, becomes anxiety-provoking, forcing your dog to cry and try to wake you up. For him, being alone is unthinkable. He may die because you are not there. It's as intense as that. His survival instinct is on the alert.

If your dog only has anxiety at night, then again, the best solution is to keep your dog with you overnight. But the best for the future is to consider using a canine behaviorist to work on this anxiety problem because, at this level of distress, the dog is not well. It is essential to help him become independent and to make him feel safe when you are away.

What are the signs of canine anxiety?

• Your dog is scratching the door to mutilate his paws

• He screams, groans constantly

• He salivates profusely

• He trembles

• He does his business (when he is usually clean)

3. Is your dog bored at night?

It's a fact: dogs can get bored while you're asleep. So they'll try to wake you up to start the game or bark outside to keep them busy.

If your dog wakes you up, the best thing to do is ignore him completely. I know there is nothing magic about this solution, and it is rather restrictive because it requires patience and tenacity. However, do not forget that your dog will remember that it needs to bark for a while so that you eventually crack and take care of him.

So, put on earplugs and close your bedroom door if necessary, but ignore your dog at all costs.

On the other hand, generally, when it comes to this solution, it is possible that you forgot some steps: your dog's needs. One fine day (or one fine night!) he will understand that it is no longer useful. You will have won! Yes!

Daily Physical Activities and Mental Activities to Be Healthy.

It is, therefore, important to keep your dog busy during the day, but also at night if Fido tends to be nocturnal: using things like toys, frozen kongs, bones, treats hidden in the house, etc. Also, don't forget to exercise it physically before bed!

4. My puppy cries at night! Help!

Puppies have different needs, both physiologically and psychologically. Most of the barking during the night, in their cases, is due either to a desire or to insecurity.

To prevent your puppy from waking up at night to do its business:

• Note what time your puppy wakes up

• Put your alarm on 30 minutes before its usual wake-up time. You may need to put your alarm on several times during the night, depending on your puppy.

• Take your puppy outside calmly, without paying too much attention

• Wait for him to do his business and reward him

• As the weeks go by, postpone your initial waking time more and more so that your puppy learns to get a full night's sleep without going to the bathroom

Why this approach? To teach your puppy that he does not need to wake you up to meet his needs! This technique will reassure him and show him that he does not need to ask to obtain it!

5. And the puppy that cries/barks out of insecurity during its first nights?

You make him sleep with you, in his cage placed near your bed. Over the days and weeks, quietly move the cage out of your room, inch by inch. Do not be afraid to put your fingers in the bars or reassure him if he is afraid during the first nights!

Also, we advise you to see if the integration into the cage has been carried out. Is the cage a place of comfort and pleasure, learned gradually, or a place of distress and frustrations?

If a puppy wakes you up at night, be patient: that is what it needs. Babies will have a harder time remembering to pee than an adult. It is the same principle as a human baby, except that a puppy does not have diapers.

So avoid putting nearby water overnight or food. Give him toys and a good cushion, that's all. The use of a cage can be effective in learning autonomy, so do not hesitate to use it. The kennel must be a safe haven, a small house in which your dog will be quiet and comfortable.

Bonus: Check Your Dog's Natural Needs

In general, and especially in the case of a puppy, it is essential to verify that your dog has satisfied all of its natural needs before you sleep: has gonepee (or poo) in the evening, has eaten enough, has hydrated well during the day, sleeps in a room at a good temperature (ideally 65 to 70 degrees Fahrenheit), etc.

You will understand: you have to find out what makes our dogs react to help them stop doing it, or at least to encourage them to express themselves differently. I spoke earlier of the fact that the dog is domesticated to adapt to the life of Man but, between us, this sentence is wobbly: if a man chooses to share his life with a dog, it is up to him understand the needs of their protégé.

And never go for fake anti-bark collars! Does your dog bark during the day? See here for other solutions to reduce your dog's barking!

Which Collar to Choose for Your Puppy

When entering a pet store, you have a wide range of choices in terms of collar, harness, or another tool for walking around. How can you choose the one that is best for your dog to walk properly on a leash?

What should you think of choke collars, mesh, or electric?

- The choke collar (mesh collar or choker):

As the name suggests, this endless sliding collar strangles the dog. It was initially a traditional training tool that was only used when the dog was trained by professionals.

Punishment, not an everyday walk.

- The electric collar (the e-collar):

This collar does exactly what its name suggests: it gives electric shocks to the dog. There are several types of collars, the one that is controlled with a joystick and the automatic that is triggered when the dog barks, for example. This necklace is illegal in several regions of the world, and many associations are fighting to prohibit its use deemed inhuman.

Why not use these collars with your dog?

In addition to making the dog sore, they create fear, anxiety, acquired helplessness, but also bad associations; for example, if I strangle or zap my dog who is barking after another dog, the association that the latter makes is not necessarily to stop barking but: "when I see a dog, it hurts."

Better Tools for Training Your Dog:

The halti (head harness):

This type of head harness can be useful in some cases, but it should be used with care. Although not all of the scientific data has yet been counted, the halti could damage your dog's throat during a sudden shock (leash, sudden blow). What you often see are dogs scratching to remove it (on the ground, or against people's legs).

Making him wear a head harness would be highly appropriate (how to put it on, wear it, and like to wear it). A qualified dog trainer could help introduce it to your dog to avoid any discomfort.

The Different Types of Dog Harnesses

Several types of the harness are available, the one with a tie on the back, the one for the car, the one for canicross, the one with a frontal tie, or even the one that grips the dog when it pulls.

• Harnesses that grip the dog

These should be avoided because they have substantially the same effect as a choke collar, and friction may damage the skin of your companion.

• Harnesses attached at the back

Just like the canicross harnesses, these allow your dog a nice pull forward; it is possible that he will pull more on a leash, a course is required. While picking up a harness for your dog, be careful so that it must be frictionless. You must keep this thing in mind that few dogs come to know to get rid of this trap by changing their body position and lowering their heads!

• Harnesses with frontal attachment

They allow for easier control because when you pull, the dog naturally turns towards you. On the other hand, certain dogs learn to shoot all the same with; a trainer can then help you teach your companion to walk well on a leash.

If your dog is short-haired, it is better to use a padded model to avoid scratches.

In Summary:

Choosing the right tool for walking is essential for the comfort and well-being of your dog and also yours. It is not common for dogs to have strolled on a leash, so you must be aware of this term and must reinforce our pet with this.

Soft and flat collars must be given priority in comparison with pointed collars and other such nasty instruments, which can cause choke or point collars. If your dog is pulling a lot, a harness with frontal attachment, and a little training, you should keep exercising your hand. The Canine Equipment, Ruffwear, and Easy-Walk brands produce good models.

An educator can help you quickly put an end to the situation so that the walks with a dog are more pleasant while referring you to the right tool for you.

• Ignoring bad behavior: does it work?

By voluntarily ignoring inappropriate behaviors and paying attention to those that are appropriate allows you to prevent the problematic habits of our furry friend from growing by strengthening them.

Note that a distinction must be made between intentional ignorance (that which serves as an intervention tool) and ignorance of the problem outright.

The principle of behavioral extinction is the "non-presentation" of the consequence usually associated with an action.

For example, if Fido has a habit of jumping on you for petting when you get home and you choose to ignore it completely, jumping behavior should (in principle) decrease.

The same is true if you have taught your dog to sit on command in exchange for a treat. After several dozen repetitions without reinforcement, it is quite possible that he will ignore your order, preferring to go and sniff further in the hope of finding something more pleasant to do.

The same goes for you: if your boss stops paying you, you will go to work elsewhere.

Note that your dog (and you!) does not produce any behavior that does not bring him anything. Here are a few ideas that will allow you to "intentionally ignore" your dog with flying colors!

Why Punishment Can Motivate Your Dog

Punishment, in the behaviorist sense, cannot reinforce bad behavior. However, punishment in the human sense of the word can.

If your puppy tends to steal your underwear and your reaction in these conditions is to run while yelling towards your puppy, which runs away, it is possible that it reinforces more and more this little habit, which becomes a call to effectively play with him.

What you have to offer to motivate Fido:

- Touch with your hands

- Speak

- Watch

If you want to suppress behavior by ignoring it, do not touch, talk to, or watch your dog.

Self-Reinforcing Behaviors

Certain actions of our dogs cannot be simply ignored in the hope that they will disappear since they are pleasant to produce.

Take the example of a puppy that eats a wooden chair leg. It is possible that your dog is eating one of your possessions in the hope of seeing you react. However, in the majority of cases, gnawing (especially in a puppy) is a basic need: chewing allows him relief from teething, gives him something to occupy himself, and lets him have fun.

Another example is for your dog to do his business in inappropriate places. Urinating and defecating are behaviors that are impossible to extinguish (since they are vital) in addition to providing pleasure to the canine individual ... The pleasure of being relieved!

A non-exhaustive list of self-satisfying behaviors:

• Digging

• Chewing

• Jumping

• Hunting

• Grouping (for sheepdogs)

These behaviors are not motivating for all dogs ... all individuals have their own preferences!

How to Overcome These Habits Without Punishing Your Dog

Since self-satisfying behaviors cannot be extinguished, the most effective and ethical way is to supervise the way in which they are produced ... In short, to find a compromise!

If you can't teach a dog not to urinate, you can show him in what context he can.

If you can't stop a dog from chewing, you can give it something to brush its teeth on.

If you cannot prevent a dog from digging, you can give it a bin filled with sand in which it can take its foot without destroying your garden.

The Cycle of Behavior Extinction

When you use intentional ignorance to reduce the behavior, you must apply certain rules and be familiar with the adventure you are embarking on, because it is sometimes not easy.

• The peak of extinction

If the behavior was usually reinforced and suddenly stopped, the individual could increase the intensity of their old habits, use a new way of achieving their goals, and even become aggressive.

For example, Brutus has a habit of jumping on his owners to signify that he wants to be kicked. Usually, his human runs and plays with him. Finding that this craze is starting to annoy her, she decides to ignore her hairy friend. Brutus disconcerted that his pirouettes do not produce the expected effect, and tries several options:

• Jump again, jump higher, jump faster

• Yapping

• Nibbling on the clothes of its owner and pulling them

• Growling

Just because Brutus is a bad dog does not mean that the usual solutions no longer work and that he is trying to get what he always managed to get in the past.

Let's take another example, using a situation that a human can experience this time. You try to open the door of your car, but it does not flinch and stays in place. This could make you late! You then try to:

• Place key back in its place and turn it again

• Push the key harder into the lock and turn it again

• Apply more pressure when you turn the key

• Try to open another door

• Pull one of the doors very hard

Finally, you kick one of your tires and take a taxi, so you don't get to work late.

Important reminder concerning the possible behaviors during the peak of extinction:

1. A variation on the same theme (try another method to achieve the same ends)

2. Increase in intensity, frequency and / or duration of behavior

3. The appearance of aggressive behavior due to excessive frustration.

A Good Method of Dog Training Under Certain Conditions

Using intentional ignorance to reduce your dog's behavior that bothers you is an extremely effective method, provided that you are consistent, use good management techniques, and teach your furry friend a new behavior (more adequate) in place of the old.

Constancy or Random Reinforcement

One of the best ways to maintain behavior (used by most canine trainers) is to use a "random" reward ratio. The animal, who cannot predict when the reward will arrive, continues to be motivated.

You can refer to the lottery to better reflect this concept: people like to play and bet because there is an element of unpredictability, which is very stimulating.

This process is double-edged because it explains the durability of certain dog habits that exasperate us.

If you ignore your dog when he brings his toys to you most of the time (which is not all the time!), he will continue to make these calls for playtime... resulting in your exasperation!

If you decide to ignore your dog to extinguish one of his behaviors, you will have to arm yourself with a determination of steel ... Otherwise, you will accentuate the problems you are having with your pet.

Use the Right Management Tools:

Trying not to pay attention to a 120-pound Danish man who pulls your clothes to invite you to play is impossible. By using certain tools, you can more easily not be absorbed by your dog friend's tricks.

A non-exhaustive list of tools to use:

• Leash for a dog that jumps on its owners

• Cage for a dog that tends to gnaw on property

• Earplugs for a dog that is barking for attention

Using good management tools is not a lazy method, but rather a smart way to conserve all of your energy to reinforce your dog's good behavior. Consult a good chapter by Nadine Caron on this subject.

Prepare For All Eventualities When Training Your Dog

To quickly decrease the frequency of a behavior, you can ignore it, while offering more interesting options to your pet. Dog trainers call this technique differential reinforcement.

We act on behaviors in two different ways: by increasing those which are desired by using reinforcement and by decreasing those who are not desired by applying extinction. By the same token, you limit your exposure to this famous "peak of extinction."

Lead to incompatible behavior; the technique consists of reinforcing a behavior that is physically incompatible with that of which you stop seeing the frequency decrease.

For example, it is teaching a dog to systematically return to its owner when it sees a squirrel or to sit when a guest enters the house.

A dog cannot run in two directions at the same time, nor can it jump and sit at the same time.

Train Alternative Behavior

This technique consists in reinforcing an appropriate behavior having the same function as a behavior which is not it. This procedure is usually used when producing self-reinforcing behaviors.

For example, if your small dog tends to bark to be hugged, you can train him to scratch your pants to indicate that he wants attention (or any other behavior that you consider more appropriate).

Reward All Other Behaviors

When this procedure is used, you reinforce everything that does not involve unwanted behavior. This technique is very effective when you are confronted with easily frustrated or excitable animals.

Dog owners often forget that the absence of bad mania can also be rewarded and brought about.

For example, by keeping his puppy busy, you reward the behaviors of research, chewing, pursuit ... Instead of behaviors of attention-seeking like pulling clothes, gnawing furniture, unrolling rolls of toilet paper ...

See our chapter on: How to keep my dog busy in the house and mentally stimulate it?

Some advice:

1. Before choosing which strengthening procedure you will use, it is important to understand why your pet does this.

2. If the function of a behavior is easy to find, it would be wise to opt for the reinforcement of alternative behavior.

3. If you quickly find inconsistent behavior to teach your dog, you can use this method. However, it requires a little creativity!

4. Generally, you will have to train and reinforce these new behaviors outside of problematic situations so that learning is faster and easier!

Focus On the Important Points of Your Dog's Training

Using intentional ignorance of unpleasant behaviors as a means of canine education is also an unparalleled method to remain optimistic and positive in the training process of your animal because it allows you to emphasize and emphasize what you like.

The human being who trains the dog also needs to celebrate successes to stay motivated!

In Conclusion:

Any dog owner can successfully use the above-mentioned conditioning techniques.

A little reminder :

• Ignore bad behavior

• Understand the function of behavior

• Be aware of the peak of extinction

• Use good management methods

• Reinforce more appropriate behaviors

Yes, sometimes it becomes a herculean task to find out if you ignore the animal in the right way, whether a behavior is self-satisfying or not, holding on if a peak of extinction occurs, to have the right management methods and use differential reinforcement programs wisely.

If in doubt, consult a canine educator in your area using positive canine education methods.

I hope this chapter has helped you better understand your new puppy! Remember that

when you feel discouraged because you are
having a hard time, we have all had the same
experiences!

Dog Training

The education of a dog, also called
training, is essential to ensure a good
relationship with its owner.

Training your dog will help him better
understand the expectations of his master,
and to promote healthy communication. Dog
training can also consist of learning specific
tricks or tasks. Different dog training
specialists can assist you in training a dog.

What is Dog Training?

Dog training and dog training are often
confused. It should be understood that dog
training is a very specific training, which not
all dogs necessarily need.

Differences Between Canine Education and Dog Training

It is very common for a master to
confuse the terms of canine education and
dog training. And yet these two terms do not
mean exactly the same thing:

- Canine education refers to the dog's
  training in everyday life. This goes
  from cleanliness to walking on a

leash, without forgetting the basics of canine obedience. A well-educated dog is often more pleasant to live with ... and happier.

- Dog training: dog training is more complex. It is about teaching the dog to a specific task. You must train a guard dog, a rescue dog, or a guide dog so that they are able to achieve what is expected of them.

The confusion that exists between these two terms exists because you very often speak of "training" a dog to designate its education. However, the term "training" retains a rather pejorative aspect when it designates the basic education of the animal.

In many cases, it's observed that a lot of owners don't need a dog training session. However, dog education is essential for any type of dog.

Why Train A Dog?

Different situations can lead you to want to learn more about dog training. Thus, it is possible to use the services of a dog trainer for different situations:

• Training a working dog: hunting dog, guard dog, guide dog, rescue dog, etc.

• The practice of a demanding canine sport.

If dog training is only useful in very specific situations, all dogs must be trained. And for a good reason, the education of a dog is essential to promote a good relationship between a master and his dog.

It is good to know that the training of a utility dog systematically involves the use of a specialized trainer. And for a good reason, quality dog training requires a lot of time and work that can be spread over long months.

Which Provider Should You Choose to Train a Dog?

It is not always necessary to go through a specialist for dog training. On the other hand, some dog training specialists can help you better train or educate your pet.

We find in particular three core businesses very useful for training a dog:

The Dog Educator

A dog educator is a specialist who helps individuals train their dogs. This goes through different stages:

- The educator often intervenes as soon as the puppy arrives at home.

- The trainer helps the master to understand how to train his dog day by day.
- He can help the master teach his simple dog tricks.

If he intervenes as soon as the animal arrives at home, the canine educator accompanies the master's in education and allows him to avoid certain errors.

The use of a dog trainer can also help a master to strengthen his relationship with his dog, for example, in order to learn a dog sport, such as agility.

The Canine Behaviorist

The canine behaviorist acts as a "psychologist" for dogs, since he helps a master to understand better how his animal thinks.

A behaviorist is often called in when a dog suffers from behavioral problems: aggression, fear, barking, destructive behavior, separation, anxiety, etc.

The goal of the behaviorist is to help a master understand the origin of a dog's behavior problem, to put an end to it.

Good to know: most canine behaviorists are also dog trainers.

The Dog Trainer

A final specialist is the dog trainer.

A dog trainer specializes in the training of working dogs. It generally only works on already educated dogs, which have reached adulthood. Very often, such a professional intervenes in a specialized center.

Generally, only professionals working with a working dog are required to hire a specialized dog trainer.

How to Train a Dog

The basics of canine education are not necessarily that complex to learn. It is nevertheless advisable to use an educated canine if you have never trained a dog before.

The main thing is to always train a dog gently, without trying to rush the animal.

The Principle of Positive Dog Training

Most dog training specialists today use positive education methods. Dog education using these methods requires various precautions:

- The use of punishments is banned; you should ignore unwanted behavior rather than punish it.

- On the contrary, any desired behavior is rewarded with treats and caresses.
- These methods completely ignore the old notions of dog training, based on relationships of domination or submission.

A vast majority of canine trainers agree that dog training through reward is much more effective and helps to avoid the appearance of behavioral problems.

Teach Commands to Your Dog

To train a dog day by day, it is important to teach it different orders, without trying to make it a circus animal! Some basic commands, such as "sit," "down," or "stay" are essential to know.

Learning an order is always done the same way:

• Gently, and using gestures, encourage the dog to perform the desired position (for example, sit still).

• When the dog runs, praise him and give him a treat.

• Repeat the exercise, and associate an order with the gesture (in our example, the order will be "seated").

• Repeat this exercise regularly, during short canine training sessions, until the dog masters the order.

• As time goes on, intensify the exercise or practice it in an unknown setting (for example, in a park) to reinforce the education of the dog.

The use of a clicker can help you educate your dog because this device allows you to emit a click (to be associated with the reward in the dog's mind) for each good behavior.

Good to know: it is never too late in training a dog. On the other hand, dogs learn much more quickly when they are young than when they are old.

The Use of Canine Education Courses

If you want to be sure of adopting the right gestures to train a dog, you are free to approach a dog trainer or even a dog club. You can take dog training courses there which will help you master the basics of dog training.

The Different Dog Education Courses

There are multiple solutions to train a dog with a professional. The courses relating to the education of your dog are optional:

- individual or collective;
- basic or intensive.

It is advisable to take a canine education course of a few hours regularly, to master the basics. Otherwise, you may need an intensive dog training course to correct early training errors.

Good to know: personalized monitoring of the dog is necessarily more expensive than group lessons in a dog club.

Where Are Dog Education Classes Held?

Based on wishes and what is concerned with us, then you can participate in training courses in different settings: in a dog club (with other dogs), at home (in individual sessions), or in an urban environment (in individual sessions).

Working from home can facilitate the early stages of training a dog. But it is advisable to quickly bring the dog into contact with other animals and noises, to get him used to the scenes of daily life.

The Interest of Dog Education Lessons

Even if the use of the services of a dog club or an educator is optional (you are free to train your dog yourself), it is strongly advised to call on such professionals.

Taking dog education lessons has many benefits:

- You avoid the classic mistakes in canine education.
- You leave on a good basis with your dog.
- You receive professional advice.
- You introduce your animal to the scenes of everyday life.
- You strengthen your relationship with your dog.

The Use of Dog Training Services

If you want to train a dog at work, it is essential to use dog training. But how can you train a dog at work?

It is essential to understand that the training of a working dog must be prepared from the birth of the puppy, can be spread over several weeks or months, can require the constant intervention of a trainer, and can be extremely expensive.

It is no coincidence that most working dogs are trained in individual education centers.

The Different Types of Dog Training

You should know that there are various kinds of dog training suitable for all trades and all uses.

For example, the trades of:

- Defense dog;
- Detection dog;
- Guide dog;
- Rescue dog;
- Truffle dog;
- Hunting dog;
- Etc.

While each breed of dog can theoretically learn the job, a working dog is often carefully selected based on its breed and physical and behavioral skills.

The trainer or dog trainer professions necessarily require specific training. To be a canine educator, you must hold a professional certificate as a canine educator;

CHAPTER SIX

Why Is My Dog Bored? Seven Ways to Occupy a Bored Dog

For thousands of years that the dog has lived with us, we have always assigned him trades in which to specialize to help us in our tasks. Dog breeds have also been designed for this purpose: guard dog, hunting dog, draft dog, sheepdog, rescue dog, or even fighting dog. Our companion, therefore, always had a daily job to accomplish. However, in our modern societies and our consumer lifestyles, we have somewhat forgotten what the dog was used for all this time. We cut her job off for the benefit of a new function: dog Our furry friend is now unemployed, and his only role today is simply to be our companion.

If you have to draw a parallel with yourself, try to imagine this (if you have been unemployed like me, it should be easy): you have lost your job. You have to stay at home, doing nothing. You no longer have any money to pay for entertainment and outings, or even the Internet or television. Imagine that you have no books, no pen to write. Imagine that you have no friends or family. Would you be able to stay all day without doing anything? With just a half-hour outing a day?

Now put the dog in this same situation: there is no more work to do. It wants more occupations, more leisure, more stimulation. The dog-without-a-job will surely look for things to do, which, for you, will be unacceptable: destroy the furniture, bark excessively, dig, get excited about nothing, cry during your absence, nibble, jump, chew your shoes, bite the tail, etc.

It's easy to understand: your dog is bored. Like a two-year-old child who has no toys or no attention: maybe he could decide to make pretty drawings on your white walls or to cook on your beautiful freshly cleaned tiles.

Does that make sense to you now?

So now, let's try to find solutions to keep your dog occupied.

Seven Ways to Occupy My Bored Dog

Let's start at the beginning and find out what activities the dog must instinctively perform to be well. There are five types:

- Locomotor activities: walking, running, jumping, swimming, etc.
- Vocal activities: barking, moans…
- Masticatory activities: eating, chewing
- Intellectual businesses: hunting to find food, looking for objects, smells …
- Sexual activity: we will not cover it in this chapter. And then, obviously, your dog is sterilized, right? ;)

On average, your dog requires 3 to 5 hours of activities per day to be balanced. Here are several ways to give him what he needs ...

Find your food!

To provide enough mental stimulation to Fido , there are several bowls and interactive toys that will make him think to release or access food:

- The Stimulo bowl by Aikiou or the moderator bowl by Be One Breed
- The Omega Paw
- The Snuffle Mat (enrichment mat):
- The Kong Gyro
- The Kong Wobbler (found almost everywhere in several sizes)
- The Planet Dog Orbee-tuffsnoopball (found in some pet stores and online)

- Ideas of bowls to make yourself:

In the same way that you get up in the morning to go to work and earn your wages to buy food, it is the same for the dog: it must work to eat! And don't be guilty of forcing it. It's part of intellectual development. Furthermore, once these different tools have been introduced to your dog, stop using his regular bowl. Forever!

Sit down! Lay down! Stay!

Your dog is intelligent. Maybe you think he's "stupid" or stubborn. No, your dog simply lacks motivation. Any dog can learn to do all kinds of tricks (noting that he has the physical ability to do them).

Learning to sit on command, lie down, play dead, walk on front legs, or jump in a circle are all examples of tricks you can teach your dog. It will then begin to think intensely to understand and apply what you ask.

Five minutes of training equivalent to 1 hour of walking. Why then deprive yourself of it? Especially since these 5 minutes of working together will considerably strengthen your bond! Nothing better to build your self-confidence and increase your general ability to get things done.

Remember that all work deserves wages! You will, therefore, have to pay your dog accordingly to maintain

Good Motivation

For this practice, you will need:

- Treats (dried liver, cheese, bacon or even his kibble if he is hungry enough)
- A clicker (it is better to test the sound with your dog before buying it, some are set louder than others)
- A hungry dog (and therefore motivated!)
- A training protocol (a trainer can show you how to train your dog well)

Move!

Physical activity should not be forgotten in everyday life. A dog usually has a hefty dose of energy to spend each day. A simple walk is often not enough to fill this need. Besides, if your dog could walk at his own pace, you will likely run behind (if not ride a bike!)

Today there are multiple canine sports that ensure both fun and physical demands:

- Harness sports: canicross, bike-jöring, sky-jöring, sled traction,

- Choreographic sports: freestyle and agility

Chew!

As you have seen above, your dog needs to chew objects. It's good for his mind and his natural chewing need. The dog has a jaw that needs to work and stay active!

Give him regular bones to chew: raw bones (patella of beef or bone marrow), leather bones, bully sticks ... It will keep him busy for a while without you having to do anything.

Don't hesitate to play tug of war with your dog too! He will love it!

Outings with friends!

Your dog also needs variety and social interaction. It is important for his well-being that he rubs shoulders with other humans and dogs from time to time. Using dog walkers will cut your day off while you are at work. If your four-legged friend gets along with others, these walks are often organized in groups, which will allow your dog to interact with other dogs and to maintain healthy links with these.

Going to the dog park or day boarding can be another exciting option. This brings diversity in places and meetings. Also, you can enjoy quiet time while your dog is having fun.

Be careful, however, to check which types of dogs are in the park before entering it. See also the reaction of your dog: does he seem stressed? Interested? Do not go if you are not sure.

If your dog tends to be reactive or stressed in the presence of other dogs, a solitary walk should be considered. At the same time, an educator can help you deal with this problem.

Seek and Find!

Along the same lines as thinking games, there are other ways to make Fido think while working on your training:

- Object detection
- Odor detection
- Treasure tracks: hide treats or their food in a room in your house or your

garden then encourage your dog to look for them. Increase the difficulty of the exercise if your dog shows himself a genius of the truffle!

- The game of hide and seek: hide behind a tree and call your dog. Reward him when he finds you!

Walk Somewhere New!

Walking in different places will keep your dog's interest in the walk. Often you walk in the same areas and do the same predictable route, which can be annoying for your dog. Bring diversity in the outings, and don't forget that your dog discovers the world with his nose! Let him smell the smells around him.

Finally, don't forget that all good behavior should be paid for! Imagine a world in which every good deed would be rewarded! With this in mind, when your dog has chosen to be calm and rest, reward him for this initiative. This will encourage him more to choose smooth versus the excitement.

It's already the end!

I hope this little guide has helped you find new ideas to keep your dog busy! To help me continue to help you train your dog for free, I need your help!

Continue to take a look in my blog section because I usually publish four chapters per month! So your friends will know which company in co Canine behavior to trust!

CHAPTER SEVEN

Understand Your Dog and His Behavior

Small dog, a large dog, junior or senior, male or female, all dogs do stupid things! The dog jumps everywhere; the dog drops objects, the dog eats everything; the dog breaks everything; the dog drools everywhere ... But yet you love your dogs! However, it is essential to decipher the meaning of their nonsense and make sure that it does not happen again. In this section devoted to dog behavior, you help you understand dogs!

Understanding Dog Body Language

We often hear it said that dogs only need to speak for us to understand them. In reality, they have a precise language, which allows us to understand them. It is still necessary to know and observe them. Ready to learn the canine alphabet?

Dog Body Language? What Are We Talking About?

Body language is a form of communication. It is silent, so it is the body itself that "speaks". For example, in dogs, you may notice that they will place their ears differently depending on the context. Body language is not specific to dogs.

Limits of our understanding

The dog's body language is linked to its inter-specific as well as intra-specific communication. It is related to his emotions. Your dog will not have the same position depending on whether he is afraid, happy, anxious, or reactive. It is advisable to analyze a situation thoroughly if one wants to understand his dog. Perhaps that is the limit of our understanding of the dog: our misinterpretation. So how do you learn to read your dog?

The Most Common Postures

• Playing positions: The dog has its front legs on the ground, and the rear end raised, often with its mouth open, it is ready to bark if necessary. He invites his human or dog friend to play.

• Posture alert: the dog is straight, ears erect, attentive, tail slightly raised. He is alert, he observes but is ready to react.

• The posture of distrust or fear: the dog will have a low tail, see put under the belly. The ears may fall backward or stick to the head, compared to usual. The dog will avoid your gaze or that of a fellow-creature and will turn its head. He can also lick his nose, and even blink as if he were tired.

• The so-called aggressive postures: the dog can have several of its postures or only one depending on its education and experience. He will usually have a "stiff" body. Bandaged muscles, his hair will be bristling. His bust will be forward, and his lips could be raised, making us benefit from his teeth. Showing fangs is a strong signal from a dog who is afraid or very uncomfortable. His ears could also be put back.

• All appeasement signals: these are the additional signals that the dog will send you to communicate about his well-being or ill-being. He could therefore yawn, turn his head, lick his nose repeatedly, walk slowly, make detours, or even lay on his back.

There are many signs of body communication, but also voice. Dogs do have a language, even if you don't have all the intricacies. Discoveries are made every day to improve this understanding. It is this understanding that allows us to be more tolerant because what we don't understand generally scares us.

Can a Dog See Like You And Me?

Does he have a lynx eye? Does your dog see colors? Or can he see you in the dark? What if you helped you see more clearly? Answers to these common questions are below.

Does He Perceive Colors?

The answer is yes! The latest studies have shown that the dog sees color, but unlike humans, in a more limited version. Indeed, it is much less contrasted than ours. The dog perceives mainly blue and yellow because its visual spectrum is smaller than ours. Certain colors such as red and green are not perceived by the dog. This is why your dog must have had trouble finding his tennis ball in the grass, even when it is next to him. The dogs, therefore, see well in color, but in less colored and less contrasted!

Visual Acuity in Dogs

Visual acuity is the ability to be able to see from afar, or even up close. Dogs have poorer visual acuity than humans. It also varies according to the lighting. You have to tell yourself that your dog is both presbyopic and short-sighted. Tell yourself that he sees blurry and can't make out the details below 25 cm, but he can't see better in the distance.

The Visual Frequency of the Dog

The eye does not process what it sees, pixel by pixel, but rather has an overview, in order to analyze more detail. This is called low frequencies (overall impression) or high frequencies (for identification details). That of the dog is much more developed than ours. It, therefore, allows him to see the movement of prey at about 1.5 km. This is also why you can watch long distance herd dogs without hearing the shepherd scream!

Field of View

His field of vision is also wider. His eyes are placed frontally (unlike humans or cats, for example), so his side vision is greater, from 250 to 280 ° depending on the breed against 180 ° for humans. This is why your dog does not need to look you straight in the eyes when you are walking and talking to him at the same time. He has a good overview and can follow you without a problem.

Predator Vision

Just like in other species of canids (like the wolf or even the fox), the dog does not need to have as much light as the human to be able to see in the dark. It will be able to distinguish a prey in the dark, only thanks to the stars without difficulty. The dog's eye is more sensitive to very weak light beams, which is only possible at the expense of colors. Behind the retina, there is a reflective surface that can amplify light. This is why, in the dark, your dog will have bright eyes if you point light in his direction. How does a dog see?

My Dog is Chattering

Your dog is chattering, but you don't know why or what to do? This chapter is made for you! It can be part of his communication. Here are some ways to understand this behavior!

What if your dog is cold?

As with humans, a dog can be cold. The thermal shock can cause tremors and involuntary spasm, which could cause them to chatter! These muscle spasms are there to maintain or improve body temperature.

My Dog Is Chattering, Is It Because of Threat, Stress, and Worry?

Chattering is part of the communication your dog uses, just like growling, barking, and so many others! So it's not abnormal! On the other hand, if your dog comes to chattering teeth, it is because the situation he is in is uncomfortable, even stressful.

Thus, you can notice dogs chattering teeth voluntarily, to ward off a threat, a fellow man, a human.

If your dog is too stressed and afraid, his teeth will chatter because his emotional state is too intense. The chattering of teeth will then be a neurogenerative manifestation. Often, this signal is accompanied by many other reactions, such as excessive salivation or the fact that the dog can urinate on it.

My Dog Is Chattering, Is It Because of Excitement?

Teeth chattering can also be a sign of your dog's excitement. It remains mental stress that the dog cannot manage. This excitement and the chattering of teeth will be accompanied by other behaviors, such as the dog which jumps on you, which barks, or which starts to run everywhere.

This excitement can be triggered by an open play session that mounts the dog in frustration, but also the simple return of the master to the home, or the expectation of the bowl. The reasons are many. In all cases, the pressure of the dog must be lowered. The excitement is natural, but it should not become problematic. An adult dog must be able to control this excitement to be comfortable in its paws.

Pheromones

Your dog may smell pheromones. These are real olfactory information, real messages for the dog. For its data to be analyzed, the dog will quickly open and close its mouth (chattering teeth). We call it the Flehmen.

If your dog is chattering, do not panic or respond with a threat. It's a natural process related to communication! Your dog is analyzing a situation that can disturb him, or he will be too stressed. You can first ignore this behavior, and if it is due to intense stress, it is advisable to work upstream, to reassure the dog. If this behavior is caused by excitement, ignore it, stop the game or the activity you were doing, make your dog calm down by diverting him to something else or by bringing him to rest in his basket.

My Dog Follows Me Everywhere

No matter what you do, your dog follows you. You are on the sofa, he is sleeping in his basket, you get up to drink a little water, immediately he gets up and follows you like your shadow. You'd like to know why—Is this a Natural behavior?

The dog is a friendly animal, which needs contact. It's natural for him to find a company. Also, the dog follows his attachment being, because it often brings him many positive things: food, petting, games, walks, and above all, confidence. Indeed, a dog will not trust that what his master brings him; he needs confidence.

And yes, by following you, he shows you the importance you have for him. You give him daily security when you are there. He, therefore, benefits from your presence by following you everywhere.

Your dog is naturally curious, and what better for him than to satisfy his curiosity if he can follow you to see what is going on?! He may be wondering if the activity you are going to do, you will share it with him!

This may be part of his "job"! Your dog may be doing guarding activities, so it continues its role once at your home. He follows you to protect you.

My dog follows me everywhere—is this a behavioral problem?

If basic, following you is a natural behavior, it may be due to low stress in your dog. If your dog has hyper attachment or separation anxiety. If this anxiety is not treated quickly, your dog could experience it daily. He could do damage in the house, have cleanliness problems, make vocalizations. He could also hurt himself without wanting to, or by hurting himself by licking sores on the legs or tail.

My dog follows me everywhere—how should I react?

If the behavior bothers you, or if it poses a problem for the well-being of your dog, it is, therefore advisable to change the situation.

To do this, start by giving your dog a reassuring frame. Forbid him individual rooms where you go (kitchen, room) so that he learns to detach from you. You can be the initiator of contacts and games, so he will learn not always to ask you. Also, refuse their attention requests, even if it means reminding you once they have turned away. Give him a toy to occupy so that he can take care of himself.

Do not forget to meet all his needs: walk every day even if you have a garden, meetings with fellow humans, and daily physical and mental expenses. This will contribute to his independence while considerably strengthening your bonds of affection.

Being followed by your dog does not matter if it does not bother you, and especially if he has no behavioral problem that would make him unhappy!

Is Adopting a Dog a Good Idea?

A final point that often comes up when you've just lost an animal is whether adopting another dog is a good idea or not. To this, there is no absolute answer, and in reality, the real question is not whether you are ready to take home another dog, but rather why would you want to adopt a new dog.

Indeed, wanting to adopt another dog should not be a "bandaid" solution, you must be genuinely ready to turn the page. You should avoid as much as possible to compare your new dog with the dog you have just lost and do not expect this new dog to behave like the previous one. You must, therefore, be sufficiently available in your head (and in your heart) and take the time to discover and become attached to this new dog that enters your life. So, therefore, you are the only person capable of knowing whether or not taking over a dog is a good idea.

In Conclusion

Losing your dog is never a pleasant step. Time will play a big part in the "healing" process, and each person will have their own way of dealing with this loss. Finally, what remains true in all cases is the need to take advantage of our dogs as long as they still share our life!

My Dog is Mean, Are There Any Solutions?

Even if you always want to see your dog as a full-fledged family member and it is impossible to think that he can be violent, the fact is: you cannot predict the reactions he will have in the face of new situations. An aggressive dog, what to do? A nasty dog will tend to react aggressively to a threat, regardless of its form. A dog may want to defend its territory, defend its puppies, and of course, defend itself. Threatening others is always a good way to try to stay at peace and limit social interactions. Defining a dog as aggressive involves many things, and can very well end up in the blood.

Risk Factors of an Aggressive Dog

There are risk factors that depend on the dog more than on the environment. An animal will be more dangerous and more aggressive, depending on:

- Its size,

- Its age,

- Its behavior history,

- Its degree of aggression,

- Its predictability,

- Its choice of targets,

- Its aggressiveness triggers,

- Its health.

This last point is vital. You must work hand in hand with your veterinarian. Maybe your dog is aggressive because of some medical condition or pain. To avoid this kind of inconvenience, it is a good idea to have your dog followed up on a monthly basis. Certain medications can make the dog irritable and, therefore, faster to attack, and even certain diets can affect his behavior. Before asking for solutions, look for the causes, whether they relate to his health or behavior. Untreated disease can quickly get worse!

Are There More Aggressive Breeds Than Others?

According to some studies, some breeds of dogs are more likely to bite and attack people or another dog, than others. There are various reasons. One of them is that several breeds of dogs were once used for specific functions by men. Some dogs served as housekeepers for their protective tendencies; others served as hunting companions. Still, others participated in dog fights, and finally, some breeds were more tenacious and playful. Even though dogs belonging to these breeds very rarely fulfill these same original roles, they still keep the DNA of their ancestors in their genes. This explains why some dogs are more prone to certain types of aggression.

Despite this, it is not fair to judge a dog by its breed. There are much better elements that betray an aggressive attitude. For example, you can study his personal character and his history of interaction with humans and other animals. Obviously, you still need to do serious research when you want to adopt a dog. A race, or a mixture of races, is not necessarily made for you or your way of life. The best way to avoid adopting an aggressive dog is to choose an animal that already has a history (refuge dog, for example) and to socialize it in an appropriate way from an early age. Above all, educate yourself!

Are There Any Effective Treatments for Aggressive Dogs?

The big question for aggressive dog owners is knowing if there is a solution that can "cure" their pet. With certain behavior modification techniques, it is possible to affect the degree of aggression of a dog. Today, it is possible to reduce the number of incidents and the frequency with which they occur, and sometimes even completely eliminate them. There is, however, no guarantee that a dog will be 100% cured of its bad habits. In many cases, the only solution is to limit the interactions between the dog and the outside world. There is always a risk when working with a nasty dog. Masters are responsible for the behavior of their animals and must take precautions to prevent anyone from being injured.

Even if a dog behaves well for years, it is not possible to predict when a maelstrom of various factors will appear and trigger an aggressive reaction. Dogs with a history of violent behavior as a response to a stressful situation will always be able to return, regardless of training. Masters should be careful and always assume that a dog is never healed, to avoid lowering its guard. Remember, you are doing as much for yourself, as for others, and the dog itself. There are far too many stories of euthanized dogs for an instinctive bite.

My Dog Does Not Bark—Is This Normal?

A dog that never barks could be the waking dream of someone living in an apartment, but it can also be symptomatic of certain problems. Before trying to diagnose your dog, be aware that some breeds are just quieter than others, and that it can be normal. It is, however, important to note that a lack of barking could betray a sickly state and that it is better to prevent than to cure and go to your veterinarian if in doubt. Also, find out about your dog's breed to find out if he is more or less likely to bark or not. If you have a barking chihuahua, there is clearly a problem.

Medical Causes

If your dog barely or barely barks, the first step is to determine if it is just a lack of interest in barking or if it is really trying to bark, but nothing comes out. If this is the second case that is diagnosed, it is quite possible that a visit to the veterinarian will help you determine what is wrong. So this is your first solution if you ever have a doubt.

If your dog has always been a big barker, his sudden silence might hide something. If a dog barks too often, he can lose his voice, like humans! More seriously, certain diseases can also affect his voice, such as respiratory problems, chronic vomiting, metabolic problems, and all lumps, traumas, and lesions close to the larynx and trachea.

A Silent Personality

A majority of dogs have the physical ability to bark, just like humans, but some dogs can be quieter than their friends. Your pet may prefer to cry or squeak rather than deliver a loud, loud bark. Other dogs just can't find enough reasons to bother to walk their vocal cords. Whatever the case of your pet, you should be delighted, since there is no problem with him. Some of our canine friends were simply born with a quiet and restful personality.

The Honeymoon Effect

If you have just adopted a dog from a shelter, you could face what may be called a "honeymoon effect." Your dog may contain his bad habits in him for the time being, while he adapts to his new environment and his new family. Then, the more time passes, the more relaxed he becomes and resumes his normal vocal personality. It was then that the owners complained about the barking noise, which definitely helps to understand why the dog ended up in a shelter at the start. You must understand that adoption is not a vain gesture, your dog may be barking, and you have to deal with it. You can always teach him to bark less often, but that's another story.

A Difficult History

Again, if you adopt a dog in a shelter, there are problems related to barking. If you don't know his history and find out that he's having a hard time barking, that may be a betrayal method. A dog that has undergone this treatment can still vocalize, but it will only emit light sounds. If he didn't want to bark at all, he could have had the bark collar treatment. Finally, in an extreme manner, the dog could have been physically abused each time he barked, which necessarily reduces his cravings. At that time, you can follow a series of exercises with time and gentle methods to restore your dog's voice.

A Calm Breed

Not all dogs necessarily bark, while some breeds have been bred for the purpose of barking to warn the owner of any threat, other breeds have not received this treatment. Some dogs may prefer to ruminate in their corner or make other, quieter noises. This does not necessarily mean that they will not make any noise, but rather that barking is not their preferred method of being heard and understood. You must cherish this silence.

Breeds That Don't Bark

Among the breeds that bark little, you can find:

- The Basenji,

- The Pug,

- The Scottish Greyhound,

- The Japanese Spaniel,

- The Australian Cattle Dog.

Among the breeds that bark very often, you can find:

- The Chihuahua,

- The Cairn Terrier,

- The German Shepherd,

- The Scottish Terrier,

- The Rottweiler.

Petting a Dog: The Right Actions to Make Them Behave Well

Everything is linked to a proper comprehension of your dog and about success in interpreting its requests and its evils. However, there are certain points that have been studied by veterinarians for a long time, and you must follow them at all costs. The subject of petting remains sensitive, but few people seem to really care. When you meet a dog that you don't know, you pay attention and try to gently pet him, not really knowing if there is a risk of being bitten or to the contrary. If your dog is your long-term partner, then these preventive measures fail, and it will be harder to understand. However, the dog will prefer this or that flattery to be such or such a place of its limbs. You have to know these training methods from day one and then carry on this throughout life.

How to Pet a Dog

• Understand your own gesture

Petting a dog is a restful and relaxing activity, which it is important to perform, whether it is a rewarding gesture or simply a means of creating a connection with your animal. You must be alert about the behavior of the dog, as you would with a human. You wouldn't go petting someone's body even when they are denying and rejecting this act of yours, so why you pursue this with a pet? All kind of petting must be accepted by your pet if you will give as a treat a gesture of appreciation then you are at loss, and you must know the educational value of your teachings.

Dogs, like humans, use physical contact to show their emotions, whether it be love, hate, provocation, or bullying. There are harsh and rude petting as well, which can damage your relationship with your pet, so you all must be very kind and passionate about caressing your dog. You should proceed with a touch which must be accepted by the dog.

• Amazing spots to pat a pet

Numerous researches have been carried on a variety of races, and it was found that likeness for a particular touch will always vary from breed to breed and in his body to favor during the petting sessions. Slow strokes on the head, shoulders, and legs tend to create signs of appeasement in animals, especially if the owner delivers them. The caresses of strangers will be a little less well-received. Avoid as much as possible, restricting the animal's movements. It can vary from dog to dog, but generally, hugs are not well received.

Keeping it on the ground, grabbing the collar, lifting its paw, and covering its snout are gestures to be avoided as much as possible. If the dog freezes, looks elsewhere, licks his lips, or tries to leave, it is a possible sign that your caresses are unappreciated. If your dog stretches with physical sessions, it means that your gestures were awkward and that he relaxes after a stressful activity. In all cases, stroking it on the chest will always be associated with a calming and restful act for the animal. Behind the ears, scratching is also always recommended, regardless of the dog.

• Petting A Dog—Some Advice

Let the dog come to you than to seek it to pet it. Dogs need time for themselves and personal space. It may take them a little while to prepare for physical contact. If you start a caress, stop and watch the dog, if he asks for more, it's that you are doing a good job!

What if your dog is sensitive and does not like touch in general, you can try to desensitize him. The exercise is simple and requires only a few treats. If he doesn't like being held by the necklace, consider giving him a treat every time you do it, it will create a cause and effect link.

Keep in mind that your pet may be sick or injured. If you are observing abrupt changes in behavior, then do not hesitate to consult the advice of a veterinarian. And if it is not a medical problem, consult the advice of a professional trainer. Explain to people who want to pet your dog which places they prefer, and that if the animal reacts negatively, it will have to stop the session. Again, it all depends on the ease of the dog, its breed, and its age.

My Dog Often Licks: Causes and Solutions

Your dog is licking, is it serious? If you find it uncomfortable to see your dog licking for hours on end, imagine how he feels. If your dog is compulsively licking, this is by no means a rare problem, but the causes are many and varied. Some of them are dangerous or hurtful, so act quickly and well. Watching your dog for a whole day can give you a lot more information than you might think. It's not always expected or imperative for you to visit a veterinary a veterinarian in order to care for a dog, but keep in mind that it is better to have the advice of a professional before trying anything. If ambiguous, then must consult a good veterinarian.

My Dog Licks: 5 Causes to Know

There are five main causes that can explain your dog's behavior:

• Allergies

These may cause licking as much as scratching and biting. Your dog may simply react to an allergy, be it food or environmental. All it takes is mold or pollen to keep your dog from feeling good. Certain soaps and pesticides can also create skin irritations, called dermatitis.

- Anxiety or boredom
- Dry skin
- A pain
- Parasites
- My dog often licks: 4 solutions to consider depending on the case

There are many products that can help get rid of ticks and fleas that infect your pet. In addition, if you find that your dog's licks are due to insects, be sure to clean this first, its basket, and vacuum your carpets and other fabrics that have come into contact with your companion.

My Dog Pees Everywhere—How to Remedy the Marking of Territory?

It is well known that dogs tend to mark their territory during walks, especially by urinating here and there. However, this is not a harmless act, and not all dogs are subject to this activity. The reasons for tagging are well defined and can be a problem when the animal begins to want to pee all around or even in the house.

Understanding Territory Marking

It is usual with many dogs to ask to raise their paws at each lamppost or to urinate on every street corner. The majority of owners accept this trend and believe that marking territory is a vital social activity for dogs. This is especially true for males. You just admit that you don't really understand the marking, but you start to ask questions when it takes place indoors. You could quickly get discouraged by the constant smell of urine in the house, or by the few puddles that appear here and there. The dog does not, in any case, think of doing something stupid. He can use his urine, or sometimes even his droppings, to mark a place he thinks is his. This makes it clear to other animals that it is out of the question for them to set foot in their environment. In addition, smelling the urine of another dog allows animals to learn more about the animal's sexual availability and social status.

Interaction With His World

Marking territory can come from a desire to enslave its domination over other animals. If you have another four-legged friend in the house, your dog may try to intimidate the competition by urinating in strategic places. It shows there is a row between different animals in your home. The marking then comes from instability within the social scale established by your dog. In order to legitimize his place as chief, the dog suddenly begins to pee to mark his territory. It can also happen when a new head enters the house, whether it's a roommate or partner, or even a baby. The dog will then deposit its smell on the objects belonging to this newcomer. The dog wants to make it clear that this house is his. This also happens when an unknown object is installed in the home (a shopping bag, a scented scarf, etc.). Finally, if your dog sees another animal through the window, he might feel the need to mark his territory, even inside.

Solutions for Inappropriate Markings

• Check his health

If your dog pees indoors, it may be because of a desire to mark his territory ... Or else, he just has bladder problems. A dog that overeats salt, for example, will tend to drink a lot, which will result in frequent accidents. to take a suggestion which you must take from a veterinarian to be sure your dog is healthy. The problem could be much more serious; first of all, you must rule out medical reasons. Pay special attention to stress issues.

Dog Psychology: Understanding Your Dog and Dog Emotions

Dog emotions: How do dogs feel?

One who is in affection with dogs can tell that a dog has a strong feeling for your feelings, and have almost a sixth sense when it comes to licking you when you are sad. Does this feeling prove that they have emotions? Is this a real interest in your own feelings, or just a natural reaction that is beyond their control?

Dogs Are Social Animals

It's no surprise to anyone; dogs have strong emotions. However, they may be different from those experienced by humans. Dogs are social animals, living in packs, which forces them to have socializing relationships. They build their own social structure and adopt behaviors that have no other purpose than that of bonding with other animals of their species. Some would say that it is similar to relationships between men. Hence the dog/master relationship. These connections that exist between animals transfer very quickly to any other group, whether there are other races of animals or even completely different beings. For your dog, you are his family.

Dog Psychology: What the Dog Understands

The dog understands a lot or instead interprets everything you do. Some of his skills would even touch the supernatural. Science has obviously explained all of these touching behaviors. The dog smells when a woman is pregnant, and the dog smells when you are sick, that's how it is, and that's it. It is essential, however, to understand how your dog feels so that he can better interact with him.

Dog Psychology: How the Dog Feels

• Sadness

When you feel sad, or in distress, the dog will understand and change its behavior depending on the situation. It's not for nothing if they're used in therapy. They are useful for people with mental disabilities, mental illnesses, but also physical deficiencies. If the known example is the guide dog, they are also used during specific therapies for autists, and certain situations of post-traumatic stress disorder. The dog becomes more submissive, will lose interest in his toys, and may even refuse to eat. He will come to see you when he sees you in bad shape and will come to rest his head on your knee. Few dogs even go to the extent that they lick the tears running down from their owner's cheeks. Your emotions directly affect your pet.

Understanding Your Animal: How Should You Talk to Your Dog?

It is not always easy to be understood by an animal. They do not understand your words but can detect the intentions behind your intonations. The important thing is to want to communicate calmly and to assume the vision of the dog. He may not understand why you want to get him off the couch where he sits so well, or why he gets scolded when he was just chewing on your curtains. We all need special time allocation of time for our pets, and they will make an effort to do the same.

Accuracy is a Must

It's pointless to build complex sentences. Again, your dog does not understand the words; he understands their sound and the intonation you use. Saying "You have to go, come home, and stop playing" will be far too many for your dog to understand anything. A simple "come!" will be much more effective. It's short, concise, and easy to modify. In no case shall a short order be considered to be dry. You can start a "come!" very gently without attacking your dog. You have to be touchy while choosing the first command. If Rex is so common for a dog name, it's because it's a syllable is very easy to learn.

With all these explained signals and commands, they will make you understand your dog better effectively and efficiently.

Conclusion

Taking everything into account, owning and caring for a dog is a big responsibility. Below is our summary of the points covered in this book:

- Understand the criteria for choosing your dog. Based on your own lifestyle and personality, decide if you want a high-energy dog, a low-energy dog, and something in between. Ideally, your dog's lifestyle and energy level should be close to your own.
- Decide whether you want to adopt from a shelter or a breeder. Both have their own pros and cons, but ultimately, choose what feels right to you.
- Know the signs of good and bad breeders before choosing where to adopt your dog. Avoid puppy mills or scams, and if you are adopting a purebred dog, insist that your breeder provides the proper tests and papers for your new dog.

- Before adopting a dog, learn how to take care of your new puppy. Young dogs must learn how to live alongside their owners, and may not yet have learned how to sleep through the night or where to do their business. Preparing for your little furball will help the process go much more smoothly.
- Help your dog understand you by using consistent commands. Train them at a consistent pace and provide an environment that aids their learning. Know what options are available in terms of professional dog trainers, should you need one.
- Provide adequate exercise and enrichment to keep your dog's life happy, satisfying, and engaging for both you and your companion.
- Above all, learn to understand your dog's behavior. Keep an eye out for signs of your dog's stress or discomfort, and make sure they are adapting to their new home and any new animals they must learn to live with. Just

as you communicate with your dog, they will give you signals to tell you how they are doing.

Owning a dog is a great responsibility. When you prepare, train, and always aim to do the best for both you and your dog, however, we are sure that you and your new friend will live together in a way that brings you all the joy and fulfillment you ever hoped for.